The Desperate Ones

The Desperate Ones
Forgotten Canadian Outlaws

Edward Butts

DUNDURN PRESS
TORONTO

Copy-editor: Michael Carroll
Design: Alison Carr
Cover photo: Saskatchewan Archives Board R-A8218-2
Printer: University of Toronto Press

Library and Archives Canada Cataloguing in Publication

Butts, Edward, 1951-

    The desperate ones : forgotten Canadian outlaws / Edward Butts.

Includes bibliographical references.

ISBN-10: 1-55002-610-0
ISBN-13: 978-1-55002-610-8

    1. Outlaws--Canada--Biography.   2. Criminals--Canada--Biography.

3. Crime--Canada--History.   I. Title.

HV6805.B88 2006   364.1'092271   C2006-901338-1

1   2   3   4   5   10   09   08   07   06

Conseil des Arts du Canada   Canada Council for the Arts   Canadä   ONTARIO ARTS COUNCIL / CONSEIL DES ARTS DE L'ONTARIO

We acknowledge the support of the **Canada Council for the Arts** and the **Ontario Arts Council** for our publishing program. We also acknowledge the financial support of the **Government of Canada** through the **Book Publishing Industry Development Program** and **The Association for the Export of Canadian Books**, and the **Government of Ontario** through the **Ontario Book Publishers Tax Credit** program and the **Ontario Media Development Corporation**.

Printed and bound in Canada
Printed on recycled paper
www.dundurn.com

Dundurn Press	Gazelle Book Services Limited	Dundurn Press
3 Church Street, Suite 500	White Cross Mills	2250 Military Road
Toronto, Ontario, Canada	High Town, Lancaster, England	Tonawanda, NY
M5E 1M2	LA1 4XS	U.S.A. 14150

*For all Canadian law-enforcement officers
who died in the line of duty*

Contents

Acknowledgements

The author would like to thank the following individuals and institutions: the public libraries of Guelph, Thunder Bay, Bothwell, and Bracebridge, Ontario; the provincial archives of British Columbia, Nova Scotia, and Ontario; Library and Archives Canada; the Department of Veterans' Affairs; the state archives of California, Montana, and Michigan; the Montana Historical Society; the Yukon Archives; Caitlin Press; Hancock House; the National Currency Collection and the Bank of Canada; Paul Arculus; Janet Callow; Vivian Sinclair; David St. Onge, curator, Kingston Penitentiary Museum; Marion Matt; JoAnn Galbraith; Tony Stewart; Halifax Police Services; and the Glencoe and District Historical Society.

Introduction

For many years the word *outlaw* would have brought to Canadian minds images of such Wild West gunmen as Billy the Kid and Jesse James, or Depression-era bandits like John Dillinger or Pretty Boy Floyd — Americans all. Canada, it was generally believed, didn't have criminals of such notoriety, or at least not as many of them as the gun-happy United States seemed to produce. Admittedly, Canada did have newsworthy bank robbers such as Red Ryan and Edwin Alonzo Boyd, but those criminals were seen as aberrations. They didn't — in the opinion of most Canadians — truly reflect flaws in Canadian society in the manner in which a very long list of pistol-packin', machine-gun-toting desperadoes laid American society open to embarrassing scrutiny.

Canada wasn't, of course, an almost-crime-free society. But Canadians didn't celebrate and sensationalize criminals. There was no Canadian film industry to romanticize and glorify road agents, thugs, and killers, or turn them into Robin Hoods. Canadians read about their homegrown criminals in the newspapers. Then, once the villains had been packed off to prison or sent to the gallows, they forgot about them. Thus, as time passed, Canadians who read American books and magazines and watched American movies and television could look at the careers, both real and mythical, of American badmen and say, "That wouldn't happen in Canada."

Then, in the latter half of the twentieth century, Canadian writers began to unearth stories that suggested people in Canada weren't always so well behaved. There was Peter Easton, the arch-pirate of Newfoundland; Henry More Smith, the jailbreaking "Harry Houdini" of New Brunswick; Donald Morrison, the "Rob Roy" of Quebec; the feuding Donnelly family of Ontario; the Native outlaws Almighty Voice and Charcoal of the Prairies; and Bill Miner, the legendary American outlaw who robbed trains in British Columbia.

These infamous characters, along with a few others, have become the "star attractions," if you will, of Canada's own Rogues Gallery. Their stories have been told again and again. It has been as though Canada has had no other outlaw tales worth telling. One might wish that it were so, but it isn't.

In 2003 I accidentally came across an old newspaper article about a train holdup in British Columbia in 1909. This crime led directly to the murder of a policeman. The story caught my attention because I had thought Bill Miner was the last outlaw to rob a train in Canada. I researched the story, and bit by bit uncovered the amazing career of the outlaw Haney brothers who left their native California to ply their lawless trade in Canada. It was a tale of banditry, murder, and dogged detective work that led from a lonely rail stop in British Columbia to a bungled bank robbery in a tiny Montana town.

The story was so rich with adventure, police heroism, criminal deviltry, and sheer pathos that it didn't seem possible it had been entirely overlooked in the chronicles of Canadian crime. But it had been. If this story had slipped through the cracks, perhaps others had, too.

Indeed, there are many tales of Canadian outlawry that have been all but lost. They span the country from the Maritimes to the West Coast, and from the Yukon to south of the Forty-ninth Parallel. Their antagonists were thieves, killers, and confidence men. Some stole fortunes. For others the swag was nothing but the grub for another day's survival. At either end of the scale one wrong move could mean death by a bullet or the noose, or a living death in a tiny prison cell.

The stories in this volume begin in the mid-nineteenth century when much of present-day Canada was still wild frontier. They carry on into the twentieth century through the Roaring Twenties to the hungry years of the Dirty Thirties. Some haven't, to my knowledge, seen the light of day since the time they were current events. They are the long-buried and forgotten tales that stunned honest, hard-working Canadians as they read their newspapers while sipping tea or gossiped in the taverns over mugs of beer. The stories of men like Frank Rutledge, whose criminal career came to a spectacular end in a Toronto jail, and William Ponton, the central figure in a mysterious Napanee bank heist, are in a way typical of true Canadian crime drama. They were front-page news, holding the public spellbound for a short period of time, and then they were gone. No novels, no movies, no songs like "The Ballad of Bonnie and Clyde." Again, Canadians don't, as a rule, make heroes out of criminals. And, of course, we shouldn't, because most of them don't deserve it. Nonetheless, we can't just put them out of mind and pretend they never existed.

It is not my intent to glorify, ennoble, or make excuses for the outlaws in these chapters. They weren't Robin Hoods. Outlaw life was mean and dirty and often terrifying. There was certainly no glory. Apologists for some of the men in this book might, with certain justification, say they were persecuted by authorities. Charles Coghlin was a victim of religious bigotry. Orval Shaw, a petty thief who had a knack for eluding and embarrassing police, saw a relatively harmless friend shot to death by overzealous officers. But for every outlaw who claimed to have been "driven to it" by hard times, there were thousands of other people in dire straits who pulled themselves out through honest, hard work. They, more than any desperadoes, were the real heroes.

1
THE MARKHAM GANG
Oath of Secrecy

*I*t is a myth that organized crime had its origins in the ethnic ghettos of large American cities in the early twentieth century. It is, in fact, quite ancient. Highly organized pirates once challenged the sea power of the Roman Empire. Pirates of England and the Thirteen Colonies collaborated with merchant barons and civil authorities on both sides of the Atlantic in the seventeenth and eighteenth centuries. In the days of the Old West, frontier towns from Arizona to Alaska were periodically run by desperadoes who hid behind masks of respectability.

There is a further misconception that organized crime didn't arrive in Canada until the twentieth century. The truth is that a gang of well-organized criminals plundered the supposedly peaceful farming communities of Canada West (Ontario) in the 1840s and actually got away with its crimes for years before its presence as a "gang" was detected. The gang's base of operations was the Township of Markham to the northeast of the muddy provincial capital of Toronto, but its tentacles reached across the province and even into Quebec and the states of New York and Michigan.

The outlaws of the Markham Gang didn't come from poverty-stricken, broken homes. With few exceptions their families owned property and businesses. Some were of solid Loyalist stock, though there were among them a few "Johnny-come-lately-loyalists" — American immigrants who moved to Upper Canada in search of free land in the decades after the U.S. War of Independence. Nor were they all rambunctious, misguided youths. They ranged in age from teenagers to men in their forties.

It is impossible to say just how many men and women were "members" of the gang, or exactly how many crimes they committed. They were so far-flung that they most certainly had intercourse with criminals who didn't actually belong to the organization. Many of their crimes probably went unreported, and no doubt there were crimes attributed to the Markham Gang that were actually committed by others.

There wasn't any individual who could be called the "boss" of the gang, but there were certainly ringleaders — among them Henry Johnson, David and Oliver Badgerow, James Green, Robert Burr, and Trueman Pennock.

How the gang came together isn't certain. Some members, like Henry Johnson, had supported William Lyon Mackenzie during the ill-starred 1837 Rebellion. A few of their families owned taverns, which were popular meeting places. Some, too, were related by blood or marriage.

What *is* certain is that they stole. Of course, they took money whenever they could lay hands on it, but there was absolutely nothing that could be carried off and sold elsewhere that was safe: clothing, tools, saddles and harnesses, firearms, jewellery and watches, sacks of grain, household items. One Markham bandit even showed up in court wearing pants made from cloth he and a pal had stolen from a woollen mill.

The thieves helped one another hide stolen merchandise and had arrangements for disposing of the loot in communities far from the scene of the theft. There was a shortage of both hard cash and manufactured commodities in frontier regions, so there were always buyers for cheap black market goods. If an honest farmer had qualms about buying stolen property, the seller could always explain the bargain price by saying it was *smuggled* merchandise. Smuggling was rampant in those days, and most people didn't consider buying tax-free items a crime at all. The Markham Gang often exchanged their swag for counterfeit money, which was circulated by "small fry of the gang." Spreading fake banknotes around was known as "passing the queer." One of the Markham bunch, Matthew Udell, was himself an accomplished forger.

The gang rustled livestock, too, and added a new twist to the art of horse stealing. An example of its technique was a raid made early in 1845 by Henry Johnson and his associates Thomas Alsop, John Hill, and a man with the unlikely literary name of Boswell Johnson. Splitting into pairs, the rustlers stole a horse from a farm near Brantford, and another from a farm near Newcastle. Then they sold each stolen horse in the opposite community. But there was still money to be made from the animals. Alsop went to the Newcastle farmer who had unwittingly bought the Brantford horse and told him the animal was his and that it had been stolen. He threatened to have the man arrested as a horse thief if he didn't restore his property. The unfortunate farmer, not wishing to have trouble with the law, gave up the horse. Henry Johnson pulled the same trick on the Brantford farmer who had bought the Newcastle horse. The outlaws might repeat a scam like this several times before finally disposing of the horses over the American border.

Burglary was the gang's preferred method of robbery, and it was incredibly bold. Gang members would enter a residence at night and rifle pants pockets, bureaus, and cupboards while the victims slept. A man might awake in the morning to find that the pants hanging on a chair right next to his bed had been picked clean of money, keys, and anything else of value.

The gang didn't just select its targets at random. Through a system of informants such as peddlers, travelling tailors, and even schoolteachers (the last were very poorly paid and often boarded with the families of their students) the gang learned who had money or valuables in the house. If a farmer sold produce or live-stock for cash, the Markham Gang knew about it and was likely to pay his home a late-night visit. Banks were few and far between, and many rural people didn't trust them.

The gang was in operation at least as early as 1841, but author-ities weren't aware of the existence of a criminal organization until 1845. There were several reasons for this. Outside of main urban centres like Toronto and Kingston there were few professional policemen. In many rural communities the local magistrate had the legal authority to swear in ordinary citizens as "special" constables to serve warrants or apprehend suspected lawbreakers. Communications were poor, so a magistrate in one part of the province might know nothing of crimes committed in another district. There was no fingerprinting, criminals weren't photographed, and outlaws frequently used aliases.

The Markham Gang's system of moving stolen property around certainly helped it cover its trail after a robbery, but it had two other factors working for it — secrecy and fear. Every member of the gang was bound by an oath "that he would adhere to their rules and never betray their secrets on pain of death." This kind of blood oath was nothing new. Pirate crews and smuggling gangs had required initiates to swear them, and they were common among criminal societies in large American cities.

Sworn members of the gang were obliged not only to keep quiet about their organization, but also to go to the aid of fellow members if they were arrested. This meant lying to the authorities to give the apprehended gang member an alibi. As a result, many of the Markham bunch escaped prosecution, and even in those instances when one of them was convicted and sent to jail, the authorities didn't know he was anything more than a lone bandit. Some of the Markham outfit were in and out of jail several times before knowledge of the gang became public.

Intimidation, of course, has always been the criminal's stock-in-trade. Victims and witnesses were reluctant to go to the authorities because they had been threatened with fire, beatings, even murder. When the curtain was finally lifted on the depredations of the Markham Gang, it wasn't some brave citizen who talked. It was one of the outlaws' own.

The gang used stealth to carry out most of its robberies, but it wasn't above resorting to violence. On the night of November 7, 1845, four gang members burst into the farmhouse of John and Mary Morrow, about halfway between Port Perry and Uxbridge. Earlier that day the Morrows had sold a team of oxen and some sheep at a fair, and the bandits knew there was cash in the house. The intruders threatened the couple with guns, beat them mercilessly even though they had given up the money, and even threatened their children. The robbers pounded John Morrow to a bloody pulp. Mary Morrow had her teeth knocked out and two of her fingers broken. The thugs even took the few shillings that were in Mary's handbag, then left. Three of them were soon identified as Nathan Case and Hiram and James Stoutenburg, all members in good standing of the Markham Gang. The fourth man, the one who had been the most vicious, was eventually identified as Robert Burr, one of the ringleaders.

Case and the Stoutenburg brothers were arrested on November 12 and then released on bail. Their trial was set for the first spring assizes. The savage attack on the Morrows attracted the attention of the press, particularly the *British Colonist* of Toronto. The press began to take note of the increasing number of robberies in the province, and of the names of the people being arrested. The *Colonist* published a warning advising people to take precautions when travelling in rural areas. None of this was good publicity for the Township of Markham or the province of Canada West in general, but it did help sell newspapers.

One of those arrested on a charge of larceny was twenty-eight-year-old Casper Stotts. He found himself sitting in an interrogation room facing magistrate George Gurnett of Toronto. Gurnett was a tough-minded old Tory and a staunch supporter of the Family Compact, the small elite group that controlled the province politically and economically, and against whom Mackenzie and his followers had rebelled. That outlawry should exist at all in British Canada would have been totally unacceptable to Gurnett. That it apparently was becoming epidemic would have driven him to distraction. Gurnett convinced Stotts that it would be better for him if he told all he knew about criminal activities in Canada West. Stotts decided that, blood oath or not, he was going to save his own skin. In return for having the charges against him dropped, he agreed to turn Queen's evidence. Soon another gang member, twenty-three-year-old Daniel Spencer, followed suit. He had been charged with larceny and with shooting a man. He would have the charges against him reduced as a reward for being Gurnett's stool pigeon.

Gurnett's constables started rounding up members of the Markham Gang. Among those arrested were Henry Johnson, James Green, David and Oliver Badgerow, Robert Burr, and Thomas Alsop. Some of the people named by the informers were found to be cooling their heels in jails in other parts of the province and were fetched back to new lodgings in the Toronto Gaol. People were astounded as the arrest list grew and the size of the criminal organization that had been operating in their midst almost with impunity became apparent.

Casper Stotts took the witness stand against many of his former colleagues. He even told the court about the rules by which the gang operated. "The rules of the club were that we were to share and share alike, and it was understood that if any man turned, death should be his portion." One by one the prisoners were convicted on charges of burglary, larceny, and horse stealing and were packed off to Kingston Penitentiary. Case, Burr, and the two Stoutenburgs were sentenced to hang for the brutal assault on the Morrow family. The death sentences were later commuted to prison terms.

In June 1846 there were more arrests. It seems that in some instances the wanted men tried to resist, because accounts say they exchanged shots with the police, but no details are given. So many Markham Gang hoodlums were being convicted that the warden of Kingston Penitentiary had to re-arrange accommodations in the prison to make room for them. The trials were stirring up political waters, too. William Hume Blake, a leader of the Reform Party and foe of the Family Compact, acted as defence counsel for several of the accused. He expressed concern that some individuals were being arrested simply because they were former supporters of Mackenzie, which made them marked men as far as Gurnett was concerned, and should not be convicted solely on the testimony of men who were criminals themselves. The press, too, brought up the issue of "the demon of political hatred." As a result, Blake was able to win some acquittals. One of the men he plucked from the threshold of prison went right back to stealing and was soon on his way to Kingston Penitentiary.

Some of the people wanted by the law, like ringleader Trueman Pennock, simply made themselves scarce. But even with a large percentage of the "club" in jail or on the lam, there were still Markham Gang members at large who weren't being sought by the police. The long list of crimes committed by gang alumni was about to include murder.

William McPhillips was the manager of Logan's General Store in Markham. Like other stores of the kind, Logan's did a good trade in liquor. It wasn't a tavern, but customers who came in to have their jugs refilled would often have a few drinks on the premises and pass the time with neighbours. Such was the case on the night of November 20, 1846. Several passersby saw men in the store, heard the sound of laughter, and smelled liquor. The next morning McPhillips's body was found on the floor. His skull had been smashed with several blows of a hammer. The store's cash box was empty and McPhillips's watch was gone. Evidence indicated that McPhillips had been struck down from behind while he was stooped over to fill a liquor bottle from a cask.

Once again magistrate George Gurnett travelled north from Toronto with a team of constables and began an investigation. He immediately questioned anybody known to have been associated with the Markham Gang, but all had solid alibis. Still, somebody could be lying to protect the killer.

For all that he was a typically narrow-minded Tory in his politics and quite condescending in his perception of the common man, Gurnett did show himself on this occasion to be a thorough investigator. He noticed a great discrepancy in statements given by witnesses as to the time of night McPhillips had last been seen alive. This was an important point for a detective trying to determine the approximate time of the murder. He had his constables set their watches by his and then sent them out to compare their timepieces with the watches and clocks owned by the people they had been interviewing. Gurnett discovered that there was a combined difference of almost an hour and a half, involving timepieces that were too fast or too slow. The magistrate also had the constables measure the time it took to walk from certain houses to Logan's store, so he could determine if certain individuals were telling the truth about where they had been at the time of the murder.

Despite all these measures, and the grilling of a potential suspect, Gurnett couldn't come up with enough evidence to make an arrest. He returned to Toronto and posted a reward of £100 for information leading to the arrest and conviction of the murderer of William McPhillips. The reward offer produced results within a few days.

One man Gurnett hadn't interviewed in Markham was thirty-six-year-old Stephen Turney, an Irishman who had served with the British army in Nova Scotia. Although he was now employed in

Markham as a tailor's apprentice, he had been a member of the Markham Gang and had served four years in Kingston Penitentiary for robbery. He often travelled between Markham and Toronto, where his wife worked in a hotel. Since the murder, people who knew Turney had seen him in Toronto buying a gold ring and rather expensive clothing for his wife. He had also purchased a brace of pistols for himself and was wearing the kind of suit and boots one would expect to see on a gentleman of means. It was all a bit extravagant for a man who earned a few pounds a month. This information was reported to the police. They looked up Turney in Markham and questioned him. When he couldn't satisfactorily account for his sudden wealth, he was arrested and taken to Toronto. His attempt to escape the constables escorting him to the city didn't lend much credence to his claim of innocence.

Under questioning Turney continually contradicted himself while trying to explain how he had obtained the money. He finally admitted to the robbery but said the murder had been committed by an accomplice named John Biggins, a Markham wagon-maker. Turney said that while he stood watch outside, Biggins had gone into the store and killed McPhillips. Biggins was arrested, and both men were scheduled to be tried at the next assizes in December.

Markham Gang member Stephen Turney on trial for murder. This sketch first appeared in Toronto's *British Colonist* in November 1846.

The Toronto press, meanwhile, was capitalizing on the story. There were sensational accounts of the murder and the investigation, especially in the *British Colonist*. In the opinions of some, the articles were lurid and had Turney convicted before he had even been to trial. The *Hamilton Journal & Express* announced: "We do not wish to prejudice the public mind against the wretched culprit by following the example of our Toronto contemporaries."

Toronto's *Globe* jumped into the fray on the side of the

Hamilton paper, using the opportunity to fire a journalistic broadside at the rival *British Colonist*. The *Globe* article drew attention to the shabby treatment the unfortunate Turney had received in the pages of the *Colonist*, calling it a disgrace and "low pandering to the worst passions of the mob for the sake of acquiring a disgusting notoriety and picking up a few extra coppers." The *Globe* went on to support its self-righteous stance by reprinting much of the information that had been in the *Colonist*.

The trial began on December 18, 1846. Turney stuck to his story that Biggins had committed the murder, but there was ample evidence that Biggins hadn't been involved in the crime in any way. If Turney was expecting anyone from the old gang to step forward and provide an alibi for him, it didn't happen. Moreover, it was discovered that Turney had hidden a stash of money in his employer's privy. Turney was found guilty and sentenced to hang.

June 23, 1847, was a big day in Toronto, for there were to be not one but *two* public hangings. James Hamilton, convicted of a murder committed in Toronto, was to share the gallows with Stephen Turney. As was usually the case with public executions, a huge crowd turned out for the show and the press made its inevitable disapproving observations on the numbers of women and children in the throng. On the scaffold Turney confessed to the murder and admitted that Biggins was completely innocent. Then he and Hamilton took the fatal plunge together.

The execution of Turney and the incarceration of so many of its members broke the strength of the Markham Gang for good. Upon their release from prison the one-time outlaws returned to their communities or moved on. Most took up honest pursuits, and a few even became pillars of society. Only one was known to have returned to prison. The people of the Markham Gang had learned the hard lesson that in the criminal world even an oath of secrecy can be false security.

2
CHARLES COGHLIN AND RICHARD OLIVER
Religious Feud

*C*harles Coghlin and Richard Oliver weren't outlaws. They were the sons of honest, hard-working Irish families. Both were young men. In the spring of 1847, Oliver had been married barely a year and had an infant child. The Coghlins had arrived in Canada about 1845 and the Olivers sometime earlier. They lived on adjacent properties along Eramosa Road, a short distance from the little community of Guelph in what is now Ontario. But the Coghlins and the Olivers didn't get together at neighbourly gatherings to share a drop of the Irish and enjoy a jig or two from the Auld Sod. The Oliver family belonged to the Orange Order, one of the strongest and most militant of the Protestant Churches in Canada West. The Coghlins were Roman Catholic or, as the Orangemen derisively called them, "Papists." The neighbouring families were in the midst of a feud that would bring death to both their doors and inflame a settlement that had prided itself on being one of the quietest and most law-abiding in the colony. Founded by John Galt twenty years earlier, Guelph hadn't even had a hanging yet.

The Orange-Catholic conflict was an old one dating back to 1690 when the Protestant army of Prince William of Orange (England's King William III) defeated the Catholic army of England's King James II at the Battle of the Boyne in Ireland. The divisions between Catholics and Protestants in Ireland had been deep ever since, and when the Irish immigrated to the New World, they took their religious hatreds with them.

Anti-Catholic sentiments were strong in largely Protestant Canada West, and with the Orangemen, hatred of Catholics was almost rabid. No good Orangeman could turn down an opportunity to denounce Papists or anything that smacked of being "Romeish." The Catholics, for their part, could hardly say the name of "King Billy" without spitting. Harsh words between Catholics and Orangemen frequently led to blows, and sometimes to the old Irish tradition of barn burning. In the Guelph area, as elsewhere in the province, the Catholics were in the minority, and it must have galled Orange hearts that John Galt had given the best location in the settlement — a hill overlooking the town — to his friend Bishop Alexander Macdonell, for the little Catholic church of St. Patrick's.

By the mid-nineteenth century the Orange Order had actually been banned in the British Isles, causing many of its adherents to depart for the colonies. One such was Dr. William Clarke, an Irish physician who arrived in Canada in 1835. He set up practice in Guelph in partnership with another doctor, but his ambitions lay beyond the medical profession. Dr. Clarke would become a force to be reckoned with in the Guelph business community and in local politics. He had a personal drive that his medical colleague described as Napoleonic. Clarke initially had the respect of all the Irish in the district, Catholic and Protestant alike. But he was an outspoken Orangeman. He sat as a magistrate, and when presiding over trials that had Catholic against Protestant, Dr. Clarke usually ruled in favour of the Protestant.

Sectarian strife was on the rise in Canada West in the 1840s. Toronto's Protestant Bishop John Strachan was strongly anti-Catholic, and his rhetoric served to further inflame the situation. In October 1843, Irish Catholics in Guelph celebrated the news of the release from prison of the Irish patriot Daniel O'Connell with bonfires in the town square. The following day St. Patrick's Church burned down. It is still uncertain if the blaze was an accident or the work of arsonists.

An insight into the state of religious bigotry can be found in a letter published in the Guelph *Advertiser* in January 1847. An Irish Catholic named Patrick O'Neil Doyle relates how he attempted to settle his family on a homestead in the nearby township of Wellesley but was warned off by a group of Orangemen.

"We're all Orangemen — we allow no Papist to live in this section of the township," they told him. They said that if he didn't get out they had ways of enforcing their "laws." If everything Doyle claims in his letter was true, the Orangemen not only barred Catholic newcomers from the district, they also burned out Catholics who were already there when the Orangemen arrived.

In the thick of all this trouble were the Coghlins and the Olivers, frequent and willing participants in public brawls. Guelph historian C. Acton Burrows, in his 1877 *Annals of the Town of Guelph*, wrote: "Whenever any members of these families met, high words, and frequently hard blows, were exchanged, the young men especially evincing great bitterness towards each other, and none of them being a very high character for sobriety, the disputes generally resulted from excitement through drink."

On one occasion a thirteen-year-old girl whose family members were friends of the Coghlins walked past the Oliver farm. Two of the Oliver boys, age ten and twelve, called her a "Papist bitch," sicced their dog on her, and fired a gun at her. The girl's father took the matter to court. John Oliver, the boys' father, denied the whole thing. The three magistrates, one of whom was Dr. Clarke, chose to believe Oliver and dismissed the case.

The Coghlins and their friends would stand at the Olivers' fence and shout at the house, trying to provoke a fight. The Olivers took them to court for one of these disturbances, and the Coghlins were fined. On March 22, 1847, the Coghlin and Oliver boys got into a scrap and all were hauled into court. William and Richard Oliver claimed they had been beaten with sticks by the Coghlins. Thomas and John Coghlin claimed they had both been cut on the hands and face by Richard Oliver, who they said was armed with a bayonet. The court fined the Coghlins.

The matter came to a bloody head the following evening. At the bottom of a hill on Eramosa Road, a little more than a mile outside Guelph, Richard, William, and John (a child) Oliver were on their way home from Guelph in a sleigh when they encountered Thomas and John Coghlin. There was a fight, which was soon joined by Charles Coghlin and Robert Oliver. When the melee was over,

Richard Oliver lay dead with Charles Coghlin's knife in his heart. Coghlin was arrested. Although many people in Guelph felt the charge against him should have been manslaughter, Dr. Clarke insisted at the coroner's inquest that Coghlin be tried for murder in the first degree. The trial was held on May 29 in a packed courtroom.

Just what had happened in that swirl of violence on March 23 depends on whose testimony one believes. The Olivers claimed Thomas Coghlin started the fight when he said "Where are you going, you Orange pup?" to Richard. They swore they tried to avoid trouble, but the Coghlins pursued them. The Coghlins argued that the Olivers started the brawl by beating up Thomas and that Richard had wielded a bayonet. The Olivers admitted there was a bayonet but said it was in the hands of eleven-year-old John Oliver. They insisted Richard was sober at the time of the fight. A female witness in front of whose house the altercation had taken place testified that Richard smelled of liquor.

Some of the statements made at the trial, as they appeared in the press, sound very contrived. William Oliver testified that the Coghlins beat Richard with sticks and that he went to his brother's aid, saying: "Do not murder him on the road." A little farther on his testimony reads: "He [Charles Coghlin] then put his hand to his breast and pulled out something like a dagger or knife, and made a jump at Richard and stabbed him. Richard staggered back a little, and recovered himself saying, 'Oh, you stabbed me.' Prisoner replied, 'Yes, and I meant to do it.'"

According to Robert Oliver, Richard said, "I'm done for," and died. Then Coghlin said, "I've fixed you." Robert further claimed that when he went to the Coghlin house and shouted out that Charles had stabbed Richard, "old Coghlin said, 'Oh, he deserved it.'"

Charles Coghlin didn't deny stabbing Richard Oliver, but if his version of the events is true, he struck in self-defence. Richard, Coghlin said, attacked him with a bayonet. He said he told Richard to drop the weapon and fight like a man, but "Richard still continued striking me with the bayonet." At the same time Robert Oliver was hitting Coghlin from behind with a stick.

"I had a knife in my trowsers [*sic*] pocket — an old jack knife. I took it out ... I made a rush at him and gave him a stab, but where I struck him I cannot tell; but with no intention to kill."

Dr. Clarke wasn't on the bench for that trial, but as the physician who had performed the autopsy on the victim he was called upon to describe the fatal wound, which he did in detail, adding that the bayonet in question couldn't have done any damage because it was too dull. Coghlin's defence counsel pointed out the many discrepancies in the testimony heard that day, but in the end the court found Charles Coghlin guilty of murder and sentenced him to hang on July 1.

Immediately, the Irish Catholic community circulated a petition that the death sentence be commuted to life imprisonment. The document received many signatures, and in June there was a glimmer of hope that Coghlin's life might be spared. But the government decided harsh measures were required to put an end to the sectarian violence. On June 25 the *Advertiser* announced "with regret" that the execution would be carried out as scheduled.

This was to be the first hanging in Guelph's history. Executions were public and always drew crowds of the morbidly curious, but this one had the added threat of exploding into a full-scale religious riot. The first man contracted to build the gallows in front of the Guelph Courthouse and Gaol backed out of the job after his life

The Wellington County Courthouse and Gaol in Guelph, Ontario, circa 1861. In 1847 Charles Coghlin was publicly hanged in front of the building for the murder of Richard Oliver. (Guelph Public Library Archives F38-0-7-0-0-67)

was threatened. A second man completed the task only after receiving assurances from Coghlin's family that no retribution would be taken against him. As a precaution, a twelve-foot-high wooden barricade was erected in the open space between the courthouse and the jail, and a similar structure across the recess between the two towers at the front of the stone court building. Sixty special constables were sworn in to maintain order.

Over 1,500 men, women, and children gathered in front of the courthouse on the morning of July 1 to see Coghlin hang. When the hangman and the sheriff brought him out, the doomed man spoke for half an hour, making a rambling farewell. He forgave his enemies and asked forgiveness of Richard Oliver's widow. He pleaded with his friends not to avenge his death and requested that his father, who was present, not stay to watch him die. The hangman put the black hood over Coghlin's head and sprang the trap. Three minutes later the man was pronounced dead. The crowd dispersed quietly. It was a clean job, as hangings went, but the trouble wasn't over.

The night before he died Coghlin dictated a lengthy statement to his priest, who wrote it down and gave it to the *Advertiser*. If Coghlin was sincere on the gallows when he said he wanted no vengeance taken in his name, he grossly underestimated the impact his published statement would have on Guelph's Catholic community. The day after the execution the *Advertiser* published most of the statement right under the report on the hanging itself. Mourners at Coghlin's traditional Irish wake would have read it with him still there in his coffin. The dead man's words were damning!

Reminding one and all that he was about to meet his Maker and therefore couldn't lie, he again protested his innocence and gave his version of the fight with the Olivers. The killing of Richard, as Coghlin saw it, was an act of self-defence. Had he thought himself guilty of murder at the time, he said, he had plenty of time to flee the country, but he didn't. Then he placed the blame for his troubles squarely on the shoulders of Dr. Clarke. The *Advertiser* editors omitted part of Coghlin's statement, explaining that: "The statement here proceeds to charge Dr. Clarke with neglect of duty in his magisterial capacity, &c the publication of which would render us liable to an action of law ... we do not consider that we should be justified in publishing that portion."

Now, to the Catholic Irish, Coghlin wasn't an executed criminal but a victim of the oppression that seemed to follow them wherever they went. And who but Dr. Clarke was the agent of tyranny in this latest sad act in the Irish tragedy? Some of them demanded to know what the censored part of Coghlin's statement had said, but the newspaper wouldn't divulge it. It didn't matter. The culprit had been named.

Charles Coghlin's funeral was like that of a martyr. Hundreds of Catholics poured into Guelph on horseback, in wagons, and on foot. They lined the way of the procession to the Roman Catholic cemetery. Coghlin's father wanted to give everybody green ribbons to wear on their arms, but cooler heads talked him out of it. Such a show of the colour of nationalist, Catholic Ireland could have been a dangerous provocation to the Orangemen. Coghlin's friends fired guns over his grave, and during the next few days they repeated this action several times until the editors of the *Advertiser* complained about the nightly gunfire.

The man who had begun the construction of the gallows received more threats. Then, despite the promise made by the Coghlin family, the house of the man who had actually finished building the gallows was burned down. Dr. Clarke threw oil on the fire when he responded to Coghlin's published statement with a letter of his own in the *Advertiser*. His pompous, self-righteous tone only aggravated the Catholics further.

Early in the morning of August 6 a new mill, in which Dr. Clarke was the principal investor, caught fire and burned to the ground. This was a serious blow not only to Dr. Clarke but to the community as a whole. The farmers of the district had lost a valuable asset to what the newspaper called "the demon of revenge."

The destruction of the mill outraged the citizens of Guelph. The community now rallied in support of Dr. Clarke and the other local magistrates. The flagrant violation of law and order was widely condemned. Rewards amounting to almost £1,000 for the apprehension of the arsonists were offered by the town, the British American Insurance Company, and the provincial government.

The arsonists were never found, but things quieted down in Guelph after the burning of the mill. A Mechanic's Institute was founded to promote local education and provide a social climate in which the various ethnic and religious communities could come together. Guelph's religious feud would claim no more victims.

3 WILLIAM TOWNSEND
Wrong Man or Master of Deception?

There was a sudden rise in the crime rate along Canada's Niagara Frontier in 1854. Naturally, the farmers and the townsfolk, many of them with Loyalist roots, blamed the increasing incidents of housebreaking and highway robbery on Yankee scoundrels from across the border. They were partially right. William Townsend, the young rogue responsible for most of the criminal activity, was born at Black Rock, near Buffalo, in 1832. His family moved to Canada while he was still a small boy and eventually settled near Cayuga. Soon after, his father died and young William was "left to the world," as his mother would later put it.

William grew up earning a reputation as a "notorious" character. He did poorly in school, couldn't spell, wrote with a coarse hand, and when he was older he read only what was called "low" literature. As a young man, he seemed unable to keep a job. He hired on with a cooper but was fired because the barrels he made were of poor quality. He got a job hauling barges on the Welland Canal and was fired for breaking rules. He went to work in a lumber mill but was often absent.

There were two things, however, that William Townsend was good at. One was entertaining people. He could play the tambourine and dance, despite having toe joints that were so enlarged they could be seen through his shoes. He could change his voice and mimic the accents of the various immigrant groups settling on the frontier. And he could sing, especially the "Negro songs" popularized by the minstrel shows of the time. He would even perform with travelling minstrel shows, blacking his face with burnt cork, putting on a curly wig, and donning a costume.

The other thing Townsend found he could do well was steal. He recruited a gang of shiftless young louts and began to loot farmhouses and waylay travellers on the roads. Townsend apparently picked up some dramatic terms from the trashy stories he sometimes read. Once, while robbing a tavern owner, he brandished a pistol and a dagger and announced, "Your money or your life!" The theatrical bandit had to repeat the order three times before the publican understood he was actually being held up.

Townsend would disappear from the district for weeks at a time, probably trying to cover his tracks after a robbery. Perhaps that was why the local constabulary, amateur policemen for the most part, were unable to get to the bottom of the crime wave. Then, on October 18, 1854, the Townsend Gang stepped way over the line and pulled a job that got the attention of the entire province, including the heavyweights of law enforcement.

Sometime after 8:30 that night John Hamilton Nelles, owner of a general store in North Cayuga, was sitting up alone in his house going over his accounts. His wife, sister-in-law, infant child, and teenage brother were all in bed. The quiet of the night was broken by the sound of someone hammering on the door. Nelles got up to see who it was. His sister-in-law, Lucy Humphries, heard someone shout, "Open the door or I will blow you through!" Then three gunshots rang out.

The women leaped from their beds and ran out to find Nelles on the floor moaning, "Oh, dear! My back!" There were three bullet holes in his left side, just below the vest pocket. Already ransacking the room were three men. Two had their faces blackened with burnt cork, and the third was disguised with a false moustache. Two more accomplices stood watch outside. The men demanded to know where the money was. Lucy said she was a visitor there and didn't know. Mrs. Nelles stared down in horror at her husband, who was writhing in agony and groaning "I am shot!" Then she pointed to a room. The robbers went in there and tore it apart but found no money.

Panic seized Mrs. Nelles. She ran back into her bedroom and tried to open the window, but it was nailed shut. The woman grabbed her baby, dashed to the outer room and, unseen by the intruders, fled through the open door. The two men outside didn't stop her.

In another room fourteen-year-old Augustus Nelles awoke in his bed to find a strange man wearing a false moustache standing over him. The man asked where the money was. Augustus said he didn't know. The bandit struck him on the shoulder and said he had better tell or "I'll blow you through!" The boy insisted he didn't know.

By now the robbers realized Mrs. Nelles was missing and decided they had better get out quickly. All they had for their trouble was John Nelles's watch, which they had found hanging on a nail in his bedroom. Before the man with the moustache disappeared through the door, he looked at the mortally wounded Nelles and growled, "Damn you, you scoundrel! You slammed the door in my face!"

John Nelles died shortly after midnight, and by dawn a hue and cry had been raised. Special constables were soon knocking on doors and searching the roads and back roads. It helped them immensely that right after the assault on the Nelles house two farmers were robbed on the road by five armed men. The farmers gave the police relatively good descriptions of the robbers, as well as an indication as to the direction in which the outlaws were heading. Naturally, they were making for the U.S. border.

The authorities soon had names to go with the descriptions: William Townsend (suspected for quite some time as being the leader of a gang of thieves), John Lattice, John Blowes, George King, and William Bryson. All were in their early twenties, except Bryson, who was barely eighteen. Bryson must have been terrified after the murder, because he tried to break away from the gang. Townsend, who had worn the moustache and done the shooting, held him back and boasted he had already killed six men, which was most likely a lie.

The police learned the gang had taken the train to Buffalo, and constables went there looking for the robbers. But the bandits doubled back and returned to Canada. The authorities got a lead on Townsend when he sold Nelles's watch to a man in Port Dalhousie, near St. Catharines. They closed in, and an eight-man posse seemed to have Townsend trapped in the bush near that town. But with two pistols blazing he broke through the cordon and escaped, fortunately without actually shooting anyone.

The constables regrouped and followed Townsend's trail to St. Catharines, where they learned he had boarded a ship bound for Oswego, New York. They telegraphed the Oswego police to detain Townsend as soon as the ship docked. Then, to be sure they got the right man, the Canadian police put Constable Robert Flanders, who knew the bandit by sight, on a fast horse and sent him around the lakehead to Oswego.

Contrary winds kept the ship out in the open lake, so Flanders was already waiting by the time the vessel docked. He went aboard with the Oswego police, but Townsend wasn't there. The skipper told them that a man answering Townsend's description had indeed come aboard at St. Catharines, but at Port Dalhousie he had jumped onto another ship bound for Kingston. The police in Kingston were notified, but Townsend was still thinking one move ahead of them. He disembarked somewhere along the north shore of Lake Ontario and vanished. It was later learned that he hid out in the home of a relative in Kingston, disguising himself as a woman whenever he had to go outside.

Townsend's confederates, meanwhile, were neither as lucky nor as resourceful. John Blowes and George King were arrested in Hamilton — Blowes in a whorehouse known as Limping Jenny's. Bryson was tracked down to a relative's farm near Lake Simcoe and was caught trying to hide in a rain barrel. John Lattice attempted to cross back to the United States and was shot dead by a constable on Squaw Island in the Niagara River.

After a couple of weeks in hiding, Townsend slipped out of Kingston and returned to the Niagara district. He might have spent some time with his mother, because she later claimed to have "secreted" him. He planned to go to the United States, but he needed money.

On the evening of November 2, Townsend and two other men stopped a farmer named Jacob Gainer on the road near Port Robinson on the Welland Canal. "My name is Townsend," the highwayman announced. "There is a reward of $1,000 for my capture. I must have money."

Gainer said he had worked for his money and wouldn't give it up. Townsend said he wouldn't take *all* of a poor man's money and persuaded the farmer to hand over $35. When the robbers left, Gainer followed them. He watched them enter a hotel in Port Robinson, then went to fetch Charles Richards, the village constable. Gainer took Richards to the hotel and pointed out Townsend as the robber and murderer the authorities were looking for. Richards should have sent for help, but perhaps he was thinking of the bounty money on Townsend's head. He seized the bandit by the arm and arrested him "in the name of the queen."

Twice Townsend warned Richards to release him, but the constable wouldn't. Then, in front of a room full of witnesses, Townsend pulled a revolver from his pocket and blew a hole in Richards's forehead. The constable was dead before he hit the floor. Townsend fled from the hotel, and the chase was on again.

A day or two later the authorities received a tip that the murderer was on a train westbound for the town of Woodstock. They telegraphed ahead, instructing the Woodstock police to arrest Townsend when the train stopped there. What happened next suggests that small-town policemen weren't always the brightest lot.

The Woodstock police chief sent his jailer, George Forbes, and four special constables to the station with a written description of the wanted man. When the train pulled in, the lawmen separated to search the passenger cars systematically. Forbes saw Townsend in the first car. When Townsend noticed Forbes looking at him, he cheerfully said, "I know what you're at. You take me for Townsend. It's true that I favour the description very much. I've been taken for him once before today. But I'm not him. I come from east of Rochester, New York, and I'm bound for the West."

Townsend was well dressed and so charming that Forbes decided the man was telling the truth and left the car. Out on the platform he met his four comrades, who had come out of the cars empty-handed. There was no sign of anyone resembling the wanted man except ... Forbes conferred with his men. What if that fellow *was* Townsend, after all? They returned to the first car, but the man was gone. While they puzzled over this turn of affairs, Forbes looked out the window and saw the man on the platform. Before the suspect could go anywhere they hurried out and confronted him.

Coolly Townsend again told the constables he had already been mistaken by police for the wanted man and had been let go. Forbes said he wanted him to accompany them, anyway. If they were wrong about him, he could always catch the next train. Townsend became indignant. He said it really was quite inconvenient for the police to interfere with a fellow going about his legitimate business just because he happened to slightly resemble some scoundrel they were looking for. Now the five officers of the law fell into a dispute as to whether they had the authority to hold him, after all. He certainly didn't *act* like a murderer on the run.

Meanwhile, the train began to move out of the station. As it picked up speed, Townsend suddenly broke away from the constables and made a mad dash for the last car. He leaped onto the back platform, leaving his would-be captors at the station. To cap off a day of bungling, the Woodstock police assumed the police at the next stations down the track had been alerted and would be waiting for the fugitive. But the police there hadn't been alerted, and Townsend made good his escape from Canada.

In April 1855, Bryson, Blowes, and King went on trial for the murder of John Nelles. There was no doubt in anyone's mind that Townsend had done the shooting, but under the law his accomplices were equally guilty. Bryson saved his own neck by turning Queen's evidence and was sentenced to life in Kingston Penitentiary. Blowes and King were sentenced to hang.

The execution at Cayuga on May 18 was, like so many nineteenth-century public hangings, a disgraceful affair. The town square was packed, and children perched on their fathers' shoulders for a better view. Hawkers sold food and liquor, and drunken men staggered about, cursing and fighting. To make things even more deplorable, the hanging was botched. The trap door on the gallows was mistakenly sprung before the condemned men were placed on it, giving them a nerve-jarring, advance taste of the last sound they would hear in this life. Then, when the pair took the fatal drop, the death hood the executioner had placed on Blowes split open, revealing a face distorted from strangulation. The eyes bulged and the veins seemed about to burst. The front row of the crowd was all men, so a constable on the scaffold told them, "Stand back and give the ladies a chance to see!" The men gallantly stood aside so the women could move up close and look into the ghastly face.

Aside from one report in the summer of 1855 that sent Constable Robert Flanders to Illinois on a wild-goose chase, nothing was heard of William Townsend until April 1857. John Iles, formerly a policeman in Canada West, was in his saloon in Cleveland, Ohio, washing glasses when two men walked in. One was a friend who was a railway conductor. The other, he believed, was William Townsend. Iles was so startled that he dropped the glass he had been washing. His friend explained that the man with him had been riding the train without paying the fare and had offered him a pistol as security against payment. The conductor wanted Iles to hold on to the gun until the man could come up with some money to redeem it. Iles agreed. He took the gun, and the conductor left. Iles sent the unsuspecting man into the dining room for something to eat. Then he hurried off to get the police.

When a Cleveland policeman arrested him for murder, the stranger displayed more chagrin than alarm. The officer told him to empty his pockets, and out came two Bowie knives, a penknife, and 14 cents. When the handcuffs were snapped on, the prisoner said, "Only a few hours in Cleveland and the darbies on already."

The officer asked him where he had heard handcuffs called "darbies." He replied, "In Canada." Iles asked him what part of Canada he was familiar with. The handcuffed man said he had been around the Grand River and London.

Then Iles asked him if he knew three men named King, Blowes, and Bryson. "Perhaps," he replied. "What of it?" Iles told him Bryson was in prison and that King and Blowes had been hanged for the murder of John Hamilton Nelles. The man gasped, "Oh, no!" Then he became silent and sullen.

Canadian authorities were notified, and the prisoner was extradited to Toronto, then sent to Cayuga. John Iles went with him. There was still a big reward on the head of William Townsend.

The trial of the accused killer of John Nelles began late in September 1857 and lasted three days. It attracted considerable attention because Townsend's notoriety had grown since he had last been seen merrily riding a train out of Woodstock. It was rumoured that before the Nelles murder the Townsend Gang had been at work in places as far apart as London and Markham, and that it had the blood of more than two men on its hands.

The Crown brought forth witness after witness who identified the prisoner in the box as William Townsend, burglar, highwayman, and murderer. The finger was pointed by Mrs. Nelles, Lucy Humphries, and Jacob Gainer, among others. The star witness for the Crown was William Bryson, who was brought from Kingston to identify his former friend and outlaw boss. All said, "He is the man." It looked as though the hangman could start oiling his rope.

But then the trial took a startling turn when the counsel for the defence brought forth witnesses who stated that the prisoner was *not* William Townsend. Among them were Townsend's mother, sisters, and other family members, whose testimony would, of course, be suspect. But Constable Robert Flanders said the law had arrested the wrong man, as did the reeve of Cayuga township and others who had known Townsend and weren't his friends or relatives.

The result of all this was a hung jury. After six hours of deliberation, seven jurors were for conviction, five for acquittal, and none of them would budge. One of the latter said he would "set on his seat until carried out a corpse rather than convict the prisoner." The judge dismissed the jury, and the prisoner was committed to stand trial at the next assizes for the murder of Constable Charles Richards.

The case was now the subject of debate, sometimes heated, in taverns, on street corners, and in drawing rooms. If the accused wasn't the villain Townsend, then who *was* he! The prisoner provided an answer in letters carried by newspapers throughout the province and in the United States.

The man said his name was Robert J. McHenry, that he had been born in Scotland, and that he had immigrated to the United States in 1837. He claimed to have been a Great Lakes sailor for many years and said the only time he had ever been to Canada prior to his extradition was when a vessel he was on was forced to find shelter in the mouth of the Grand River during a storm. At the time of the murders in 1854 he said he had been in California looking for gold, and could prove it. He was scornful of the seven jurors who had voted for his conviction and predicted that "as ignorant as a Townsend juror" would become a popular proverb.

The public and the press began taking sides. Toronto's *Globe* deplored the idea that a man should be persecuted because he looked like a notorious villain. Bets were laid on whether the jury would decide the man was Townsend or McHenry, and editors expressed disgust at learning that even government officials were placing wagers. Both prosecution and defence used the interim to line up more witnesses until the sheriff's list had 162 names. The defence sent for people from as far away as California and even offered to bring "McHenry's" parents from Scotland, but he wouldn't agree to that.

The trial began in Merrittsville (now Welland) on March 26, 1858, and continued until April 5. The courtroom was filled to capacity every day, and the streets outside the building resembled a rowdy waterfront. Drunken arguments between the "Townsend" men and the "McHenry" men escalated into fistfights. Pickpockets had a field day. A Thorold miller lost $700 when a pocket was neatly sliced off his coat without his even noticing. Between hearings the prisoner was kept in the town jail, and he cursed the "damned swamp angels" (a nickname for the inhabitants of the town) who came to gawk at him.

The trial wasn't about the guilt of William Townsend. Eyewitnesses had seen him shoot Richards. The trial was to determine the identity of the man in the dock. As one witness put it, "I should not think it was a disgrace to the family if Townsend was hung, because I think he deserves it [but] the prisoner is not at all like Townsend."

There was considerable testimony concerning Townsend's appearance and that of the prisoner. Some people said that small scars on the prisoner exactly matched those of Townsend. Others said they didn't. Townsend's mother and others testified that Townsend had a small anchor and his initials tattooed on his arm. The prisoner had no tattoos, but a doctor said that simple India ink tattoos were easily removed. The prisoner had neat penmanship and not the "coarse hand" of Townsend.

At times the exchanges became nasty. The prisoner's counsel asked John Iles if he hadn't "identified" an innocent man just so he could collect the reward. The Crown suggested the prisoner was being protected by Townsend's "notorious" friends and that the accused couldn't make up his mind whether he was English, Scottish, or American.

Some of the witnesses produced by the defence to prove the accused wasn't Townsend didn't paint a flattering picture of the prisoner's background. One said "McHenry" had been in trouble once for stabbing a shipmate. Others said they had known him by various names, including "Crockett."

Through it all the prisoner was cool-headed and sometimes even jocular. He did lose his composure once when the Reverend William Hawe was on the stand. Townsend had once worked in Hawe's sawmill, and the reverend said he had placed his house in "a state of defence" upon hearing a rumour the Townsend Gang intended to rob him. He positively identified the prisoner as William Townsend. The accused man stood up, placed a candle near his face, and demanded, "Take off your goggles and look at me!"

For the jury the clinching argument had to do with the prisoner's feet. Everyone agreed that Townsend had abnormally large joints in his toes. "McHenry's" feet had nothing unusual about them. The weary jurors retired on April 5 and on April 6 returned with their verdict. "The prisoner is Robert J. McHenry and we find him not guilty."

McHenry was released on £100 bail on the condition he be available to stand trial again for the Nelles murder should the Crown decide to reopen that case. But there never was a third trial. Robert J. McHenry — and William Townsend — vanished from history.

Many questions remained unanswered. Why did "McHenry" seem so shaken at the news that Blowes and King had been hanged? Or had Iles been lying? Why did close associates like Bryson identify him as Townsend? How, if his only visit to Canada had been a few hours at the mouth of the Grand River, did he pick up colloquialisms like "darbies" and "swamp angels"? Above all, why did he wait so long to identify himself as Robert J. McHenry of Scotland?

Some people believed that William Townsend, a master of mimicry and disguise, put on an act and had altered his appearance enough to convince witnesses he was someone else. Canadian historian W. Stewart Wallace reviewed the case for his 1931 book *Murders and Mysteries* and came to a different conclusion.

Wallace believed that the man in the prisoner's box was neither Townsend *nor* McHenry. He came across stories that said Townsend hid with family members for two years after the murders, then fled to the United States and even fought in the Civil War, but never returned home.

As for "McHenry," Wallace felt the man knew too much about Canada not to have spent time there before his arrest. Wallace corresponded with people in the part of Scotland McHenry claimed to have come from and learned that none of the McHenry families there could claim the man who was on trial in Canada West in the 1850s. A possible explanation, Wallace suggests, is that the man who called himself McHenry *was* born in Scotland and that he sailed to Canada with the British army and then deserted and ran to the United States. He bore some resemblance to Townsend and had the misfortune to be mistaken for the murderer by Iles. The man didn't give his real name because he could then be charged with desertion for which he could be shot. He fully expected to walk away from the first trial but was forced to use an alias when faced with the second trial. The man had obviously used more than one alias in the United States and undoubtedly knew of a McHenry family back home. That could explain why he couldn't allow his counsel to send for his parents.

That is all conjecture, of course. The bottom line is, whatever the identity of the man in the prisoner's box, William Townsend got away with murder.

4 FRANK MEEKER
A Year Plus a Day

*C*harles Leavitt of Buffalo, New York, and Frank Meeker of Cleveland, Ohio, were drinking in the Senate Saloon on King Street in Toronto on the evening of March 9, 1874. Both men had revolvers in their pockets. Both were in possession of burglar tools. The twenty-two-year-old Americans hadn't known each other long; they had met only weeks earlier in Buffalo. But they did have something in common. They were both sons of respectable, law-abiding parents, and they were both criminals. Meeker was the more professional of the pair. He had a long record of offences in the United States and was a suspect in the shooting death of an American deputy. They were in Canada for what Leavitt would later tell police was "amusement." That amusement, as it turned out, involved looting the homes and businesses of the unsuspecting citizens of Ontario. Meeker and Leavitt had already made the acquaintance of several underworld characters in Toronto and Hamilton, including at least one other fugitive from American police.

The two burglars left the Senate late in the evening, walked to Yonge Street, and headed north, looking for a place to rob. Meeker had said a shop would be the best bet, because there would likely be cash on the premises. The night was cold, so they stopped occasionally to warm and refresh themselves in drinking establishments. It was well into the small hours of Tuesday morning, March 10, when they stood at the intersection of Yonge and Bloor streets in what was then the village of Yorkville. On the northwest corner, somewhat set back from the street, was just the sort of mark they were looking for: the butcher shop and home of the Dain family. Inside, three brothers — James, Joseph, and Major John Dain — and their mother, Sarah, slept in the family quarters on the second and third floors. It was rumoured they kept large sums of cash on hand for the purchase of livestock.

The burglars went through the gate to a kitchen door that was well hidden in shadow. They tried the door, but the lock was too good for their tools. Meeker jimmied a small window, climbed in, and opened the door to admit Leavitt. They passed through the kitchen to a sitting room where the coal stove was still warm. Leavitt was half frozen from the long hike up Yonge Street, so he sat and made himself comfortable by the stove. Meeker, ever the professional, took off his coat and boots so he could creep about more quietly, and gave them to Leavitt to hold. A quick inspection of the ground floor revealed nothing of interest, so Meeker went to the stairway and started up. Leavitt later testified that he heard the creak of the stairs under Meeker's feet. So did someone else.

Joseph Dain, age thirty, awoke to see the shadowy form of a man standing in his bedroom, rifling his pants pockets. Leaping from his bed, Dain cried out to his older brother in the room above that there was a thief in the house. The intruder fled as Dain threw a chair at him. The chair missed its target and crashed against a wall. Dain, barefoot and dressed only in his nightshirt, raced down the stairs after the burglar, calling to his brother, "Maj! Maj!" From upstairs Major John Dain shouted to his brother to hold on to the villain, that he was coming to help. But as he dashed down the stairs in the darkness he tripped over the fallen chair.

When he heard the racket upstairs, Leavitt made a hasty exit from the house, still clutching Meeker's boots and coat. He ran across Bloor Street, where he slipped and fell in the snow, scratching his face as he hit the ground. The Dains' servant girl, watching from an upstairs window, saw him scramble to his feet and take off down Yonge Street, leaving the coat and boots where they had fallen.

Meeker escaped from the house and ran west on Bloor, with Joseph Dain hot on his heels. Dain was barefoot, Meeker in his socks. Meeker had stepped on something sharp and was leaving bloody footprints in the snow. Suddenly, he turned and pointed his revolver at Dain, warning him to stop. When Dain kept coming, Meeker fired twice, missing both times. Meeker started running again, but Dain tackled him and the two men grappled. Then Meeker fired again, putting a bullet into Dain's stomach. Meeker limped off into the night as Joseph Dain crumpled to the ground. When Major John Dain came across him moments later, Joseph cried, "Maj! Maj! I am shot! I am dying!"

As John picked up his brother to carry him back to the house, a young man ran up and asked what all the excitement and shooting was about. John said that someone had just shot his brother. The young stranger helped him carry Joseph into the house. There, in the light, the servant girl saw that the Good Samaritan had an abrasion on his face and snow on the back of his coat as though he had fallen. At the sound of the shots Leavitt had turned around and gone back to the scene of the crime, anxious to know what had happened. Having seen Meeker's bloody handiwork, and with the Dain household in shock and confusion, he slipped away. He had plenty to worry about. If Dain died, there would be a murder charge and an accomplice would hang right alongside the actual killer.

Doctors removed the bullet from Dain's abdomen, but there was a lot of internal damage. There wasn't much surgeons could do for a man who had been gut-shot, and they held out little hope for Dain's recovery. A $1,000 reward was offered for information leading to an arrest and conviction. Toronto's *Globe* ran an editorial praising Dain for his courage but calling him foolhardy for going after the criminal unarmed. The article called on householders to arm themselves in defence of their homes. It urged the law to apply the lash to those convicted of "burglarious outrage," especially with so many American criminals crossing the border in search of "fresh fields."

While Dain clung to life police officers took up the hunt. They found the discarded boots and coat and a revolver with three empty chambers. The police eventually traced the coat to a tailor in Cleveland, who gave the name of the man for whom he had made it — Frank Meeker. Constables followed the bloody footprints to the home of the owner of the Senate Saloon. That man claimed someone had broken into his house and stolen a coat and a pair of boots. He said the intruder had evidently cleaned and bandaged a wound and helped himself to food and liquor. The saloon owner was known to associate with thugs, but there was no way to prove he had willingly assisted a fugitive. But the police did get enough information from the petty crooks of the Toronto underworld to come up with the names Leavitt and Meeker. Within twenty-four hours of the shooting Leavitt was arrested in a Hamilton hotel. The Dain family and the servant girl identified him as the man who had been at the house.

At first Leavitt denied knowing Meeker, but there was overwhelming evidence that the two had been regular drinking buddies in Toronto saloons, though they had used a variety of aliases. Then Leavitt admitted to participating in the burglary but said he didn't know his companion's real name. Nor did he know where the suspect was from or where he might have gone. Leavitt was convicted on charges of robbery and attempted murder and was sentenced to life in Kingston Penitentiary.

Meanwhile, Meeker had travelled to Cayuga in Haldimand County, where he spent a night in a hotel and was thwarted in an apparent attempt to burglarize the room of another guest. He evaded paying his bill by checking out through a window. Meeker made it to the United States, going first to Cleveland, then Chicago. There he boasted to another criminal, a pickpocket named John Papes, that he had gotten away with shooting a man in Canada. Papes loaned Meeker some money to go to South America, where he felt he would be safe from the long arm of British justice, but apparently the loan wasn't enough. Meeker and another man were caught pulling an armed robbery in Big Bend, Indiana. On June 8, 1875, under the alias Louis Armstrong, he was sentenced to five years in Indiana State Penitentiary in Michigan City. Not long after that Papes was behind bars in Kingston, where he made the acquaintance of none other than Charles Leavitt. Now Leavitt knew where Meeker was, but he still wasn't talking.

To the Canadian public it appeared that the man who had shot Joseph Dain had made a clean escape. But Detective John Wilson Murray wasn't about to throw in the towel. Newly appointed to the Department of Justice of the Province of Ontario, thirty-five-year-old, Scottish-born Murray was on his way to becoming one of

Canada's greatest detectives. He had a tendency to embellish the accounts of his exploits, but he was a tenacious manhunter with a lot of patience and experience. Murray said he would find Meeker, or whatever the man called himself, if it took twenty years. The detective's determination to solve the case hardened when a little over a year after Joseph Dain was shot, he died. Under British law, if the victim of a violent assault survived for more than a year and a day, the assailant couldn't be hanged for murder. But that person could still be sent to prison. Murray had begun his career as a detective in the United States just after the Civil War and had been in the business long enough to know that men like Frank Meeker sooner or later landed in prison somewhere.

The detective had the description of the man who had been seen in Toronto with Charles Leavitt, and he sent it to all his contacts in the United States. Whenever Murray had to go to a Canadian or American city on official business, he visited jails and talked to police chiefs and wardens, comparing the description of Meeker with those of men who had been arrested since the time of the Dain shooting. In 1877 he came across a report on one Louis Armstrong who was doing time in Indiana State Penitentiary. The description of Armstrong fitted that of Meeker perfectly.

Informing his superiors that he had a good idea where the killer of Joseph Dain was, Murray had extradition papers drawn up. In June he went to Michigan City, Indiana, stopping in Cleveland to pick up a police detective who knew Frank Meeker by sight. The identification was positive. Murray, as the official representative of the Canadian government, asked that Meeker be turned over to him to stand trial for a murder committed in

John Wilson Murray, Canada's "Great Detective." His search for Frank Meeker ended in an American prison. (Library and Archives Canada, Amicus 2373268)

Canada. This procedure was in accordance with the Webster-Ashburton Treaty signed by Great Britain and the United States. According to the *Globe*, it was the first time since Confederation that the Canadian government had asked the American government to hand over a prisoner.

The Americans were reluctant. They were concerned that if Meeker were acquitted in Toronto he would be released. It took some argument for the Canadians to convince them that Frank Meeker would never breathe free air in Canada. Then the Americans expressed concern that Frank's brother, Charlie, also a known desperado, would get together a gang of crooks who held the Meeker boys in high regard and try to pull a rescue before the train got to Canada. But if such an operation was planned it was never put into effect.

On June 19, 1877, the State Department in Washington, D.C., issued a warrant surrendering Meeker to Murray. Meeker was being held in the Indianapolis jail pending the outcome of the extradition hearing. When Murray went to the jail to take custody of him, he found the place in an uproar. Meeker was on a second-floor balcony above the cells, armed with a club and threatening to brain anyone who came near him.

"I'll kill the first bastard that sets foot on these stairs!" he snarled.

The sheriff had a gun aimed at him and threatened to shoot him if he didn't drop the club and come down.

"Shoot and be damned!" Meeker replied. "I'd rather be shot here than hung in Canada!"

Murray went halfway up the stairs and told him, "Frank, you won't be hung. The man lived over a year. You know you've got to come. You could try to kill me, but you would go just the same."

After a few tense moments, Meeker said, "Murray, I have no fit clothes. I am not going like a pauper to Canada. I am a gentleman."

Murray told the club-wielding convict that the sheriff had a suit of clothes for him, and Meeker gave up his weapon. Still, on the way through the office the "gentleman" spat at the sheriff and cursed him thoroughly.

Murray and Meeker took the train to Buffalo, and at Lewiston, New York, they boarded a boat for Toronto. As the steamer passed Fort Niagara, Meeker saw the American flag waving in the breeze and raised his manacled hands in a salute.

"God bless it!" he said melodramatically. "I suppose it's the last time I ever shall see it. Goodbye! I'd rather I was dying for it than for what I am."

He was still convinced he was going to be hanged. Murray knew that Meeker wouldn't hang, but he still had the problem of getting enough evidence for a conviction. A lot of people had seen Leavitt and Meeker together in Toronto, but only Charles Leavitt could place Meeker in the Dain house the night of the shooting. Leavitt was serving a life sentence and was therefore considered "dead in the eyes of the law." He couldn't testify. He had so far refused to talk about Frank Meeker with his father, the warden, or any of the detectives sent to question him. Now John Murray went to him with a deal. The Canadian government would commute his life sentence to ten years, thus making him eligible to testify in court, if he would tell the whole truth about what had happened that March night. Leavitt jumped at the opportunity.

The trial was held in January 1878. Leavitt identified Frank Meeker as the man who had broken into the Dain house with him. Meeker jumped up in court and cried, "You traitor! I will kill you in this world or the next!"

Meeker's defence counsel tried to make Leavitt the one who had done the shooting, but the servant girl had seen him slipping in the snow with the extra coat and boots, and he hadn't left any bloody footprints that night. Meeker's lawyer also brought forth witnesses who claimed Frank had been in Detroit at the time of the shooting, but too many other people had seen him in Toronto. It took the jury only a half-hour to reach a verdict of guilty. Frank Meeker was sentenced to fourteen years in Kingston Penitentiary.

After Meeker's conviction, the Canadian government pardoned Charles Leavitt. The authorities were concerned that as a "stool pigeon" he wouldn't live long, locked up in the same prison as Frank Meeker. Leavitt went back to Buffalo, but the chief of police there ran him out of town as an undesirable. Frank Meeker served five and a half years in hellish Kingston Penitentiary, then was pardoned and went home to Cleveland. It isn't known if he ever tried to get even with Leavitt. Perhaps, in those long years of hard labour and enforced silence, he eventually understood that instead of harbouring a desire for vengeance, he should have feelings of gratitude — to Joseph Dain for clinging stubbornly to life for more than a year and a day.

5
WILD IN MICHIGAN
Lynching in the North Woods

In the last half of the nineteenth century, the timber camps of northern Michigan drew many Canadians for the simple reason that the Americans paid better wages. A dollar a day was no king's ransom, but it was better than the $4 a month a man could earn in the Canadian woods. The camps were rough, primitive shanties where a man was respected for two things: his ability to handle an axe and a saw and his prowess with his fists and boots. Fellers (so called because they felled trees; they didn't refer to themselves as lumberjacks) had to be able to stand up to long hours of brutal, dangerous work. Fighting wasn't permitted in camp or on the job, but at times rival timber gangs would clash over the right to cut trees in a disputed area. Then the woods became savage battlegrounds as men clubbed, punched, and kicked until one side was subdued or put to flight.

In the spring the fellers came out of the woods and descended on towns like Bay City, Saginaw, and Menominee, making them as wild and woolly as any Old West cowtown. They headed for red-light districts with names like Hell's Half Mile, the Catacombs, and Block O'Blazes in search of women, whiskey and, in many cases, a damn good fight. For that was the true measure of a man in the fellers' world: to drink an ocean of popskull whiskey and then get into a bare-knuckle, rib-cracking, saloon-wrecking battle royal. Any man who wouldn't stand toe to toe with another man and slug it out simply didn't belong in that part of the country.

One of the most formidable brawlers was Joe Fournier. Born in Quebec in 1845, Joe went to Michigan after the Civil War and quickly rose to the rank of camp boss. He so impressed the rugged timbermen with his skills with the axe and saw that they composed ballads about him. These ballads, some folklorists believe, inspired Canadian-born journalist James H. MacGillivray to write the first Paul Bunyan stories.

Fournier was renowned for his ferocity in barroom donny-brooks. These were no-holds-barred free-for-alls that included eye-gouging, head-butting, nose-biting, and stomping with hobnailed boots. (A man who had had his face stomped with those boots was said to have "logger's smallpox.") Fournier could kick high enough to plant the marks of his boots in a saloon ceiling. And, it was said, he had a double row of teeth that he used to bite chunks out of bars, saying, "Dat Joe Fournier, hees mark!"

Once Fournier's fame as a fighter was established few men were willing to take him on. But one day in the 1870s Joe got into a battle with another Canadian legend of the Michigan lumber camps, Silver Jack Driscoll. Driscoll was born in Lindsay, Ontario, in 1853. He had been in the Michigan woods since the age of sixteen. Like Fournier, he was widely known as a skilled feller and a fearsome brawler. Driscoll also served two terms in prison for robbery, though it was possible he was framed. There were times when it would have been to a rival timber boss's advantage to have Silver Jack Driscoll out of the way.

The day Fournier and Driscoll squared off in the Red Keg Saloon in what is now the town of Averill, Michigan, saw a fight that inspired songs, poems, and even a painting by Detroit artist Max Gerger. Any man who was there to witness it considered himself privileged, and many a feller would lie and say, "I was there," just to gain the respect of his peers. The Canadian from Ontario and the Canadien from Quebec had no animosity towards each other. It was simply a matter of two heavyweights with reputations finding themselves face-to-face in the same bar. Nature had to take its course. Exactly who won this clash of the titans has been lost to history. In one version the men battled for an hour before Silver Jack dropped Joe with a thundering blow to the solar plexus. In another tale Fournier hammered Driscoll until Jack threw in the towel. In both versions the two combatants ended the day by drinking — a lot — to each other's health.

After his Fight of the Century with Driscoll, Fournier didn't get to enjoy his fame for long. On November 11, 1875, he was murdered in Bay City when a man he had bested in a fight earlier in the day struck him on the head with a mallet. Silver Jack Driscoll, remarkably enough, died in his sleep on April 1, 1895.

Two other Canadians who helped make the Michigan timber towns wild were cousins Frank McDonald and John McDougal. The "McDonalds," as they came to be known, left their home in Pictou, Nova Scotia, sometime in the late 1870s and turned up in Menominee, Michigan — a town that was both a timber centre and a port. The boys soon gained a reputation for being hellions when they got into the booze. In 1880, when Frank was twenty-two and John twenty-six, they were arrested by Sheriff Julius Reprecht for being drunk and disorderly and spent three days in the town jail. In a community that was accustomed to carousing, brawling fellers and sailors, the behaviour of the McDonalds must have been more than a little beyond the pale for the sheriff to feel they needed a few days in the hoosegow.

The McDonalds didn't take kindly to being locked up, so upon their release they swore they would get even with the sheriff. They went to work for a local lumber company, and a few days later got drunk and raised so much hell that their boss sent for the sheriff. This, of course, was just what the McDonalds wanted. They lay in wait for Sheriff Reprecht and beat him senseless.

Canadian cousins Frank McDonald and John McDougal, lynched by a vigilante mob in Michigan. (Menominee [Michigan] County Historical Society Research Center)

Reprecht dragged himself back to town and deputized George Kittson, one of the biggest, toughest men in Michigan, to go after the McDonalds. Frank and John weren't expecting the sheriff to respond so soon after the drubbing they gave him, and they certainly weren't expecting the human mountain that was George Kittson. Kittson dragged the unruly pair back to jail in chains. They were sentenced to eighteen months in prison for resisting arrest and assaulting an officer of the law.

A year later the McDonalds were out and thirsting for revenge. They headed straight for Menominee, looking for Sheriff Reprecht. Julius Reprecht, however, was no longer sheriff and had left town. So the McDonalds went on a bender and decided they would vent their wrath on George Kittson.

They didn't find big George, but on September 26, 1881, they encountered his brother, Norman, tending bar in the Montreal House. The McDonalds taunted Norman with grim promises of what they were going to do to George when they found him, but Norman wouldn't rise to the bait. When they couldn't goad Norman Kittson into a fight, the drunken cousins lurched off to a whorehouse called the Three Chimneys just a short distance away. There they found a third Kittson brother, Billy. The McDonalds started playing the same game with Billy that they had tried on Norman, and this time it worked.

Billy was just as drunk as they were, and soon he was in a shouting match with the McDonalds. He grabbed a bottle of whiskey and smashed it over Frank's head. Then he staggered out the door, apparently heading for the Montreal House. The liquor- and fury-maddened McDonalds were close behind him.

Norman Kittson was standing just outside the saloon when he saw his brother coming up the street with the McDonalds following him. He called a warning, but Billy scoffed, "I'm not afraid of those sons of bitches."

"Don't do nothin', boys!" Norman Kittson shouted at the McDonalds. The words were barely out of his mouth when John seized a peavey, a pole used by loggers, and took a vicious swing at Billy, sending him sprawling. Billy was on his hands and knees, dazed. Suddenly, Frank had a knife in his hand and drove it into Billy's back. Norman ran to Billy's assistance, but Frank slashed at him with the knife, cutting him on the neck and knocking him to the ground. Billy struggled to his feet, but Frank stabbed him again, this time in the head. Norman pulled a gun and opened fire. One of the slugs tore through Frank's calf. With Norman clearly holding the advantage, the McDonalds fled. They stole a horse and rig and went in search of the doctor for Frank's leg. Billy Kittson staggered into the Montreal House, ordered a drink, then collapsed, dead!

News of the killing raced through town. The new sheriff, Dave Barclay, went to the doctor's office and found that the McDonalds had been there to have Frank's leg bandaged, and then had left in a hurry. The sheriff caught up with them outside town and arrested them for murder.

The next day there was a coroner's inquest into the death of Billy Kittson, and the town was in an ugly mood. A crowd of men who attended the inquest, muttering the whole time about lynching, crossed the river to the town of Marisette when it was over. They filled up on free liquor in Forvilly's Hotel while Max Forvilly, the owner, told them the McDonalds deserved to be the guests of honour at a necktie party.

That night a drunken mob, led by Forvilly, stormed the Menominee jail. They battered down the door with a timber and shoved the two deputies on guard duty out of the way. Sheriff Barclay was nowhere to be found. His absence from the jail in the middle of such a volatile situation never was satisfactorily explained.

One of the vigilantes found the keys to the McDonalds' cell and opened the door. Frank and John fought like cornered animals. From somewhere Frank produced a knife and stabbed one of his attackers, but another vigilante struck him down with an axe. Then the vengeful mob dragged the prisoners outside.

Lynching was almost unheard of in the McDonalds' native Canada, but in the United States it was an all too common form of "justice." What happened in Menominee that September night in 1881, however, was ghastly even by the crude standards of frontier America.

John, still struggling, was thrown over a gate so that his neck was caught between two posts. He was stretched until it was almost broken. Then he was released and dumped on the ground. One of the McDonalds begged for a priest, and a bystander ran to get

Father François Heliard. When the priest arrived, the two victims were lying on the muddy street tied by their necks to the back of a horse-drawn wagon. The priest tried to reason with the mob, but to no avail. The vigilantes pushed him into a gutter and spat on him. Father Heliard warned them that every man who took part in the lynching would die with his boots on. The driver of the wagon cracked his whip, and the horse raced down the road. Frank McDonald and John McDougal, dragged behind by their necks, were effectively "hanged." People cheered as the bodies were dragged up and down the street, and boozed-up spectators kicked at them and stomped them with their hobnailed boots.

The Canadian cousins were dead, but the night's entertainment wasn't over. The mob strung the bodies up on a railway crossing sign and pelted them with rocks and debris. Then they cut them down and hauled them to the Three Chimneys where, in the booze-fogged opinion of the crowd, the trouble had all started. The vigilantes put the shattered corpses into a couple of beds and forced some of the prostitutes to get in bed with the dead men. When they had enough of terrorizing the unfortunate women, the vigilantes hauled the bodies back outside and hung them yet again, this time to a tree right by the Three Chimneys. Then they set fire to the brothel and burned it to the ground.

The next morning the bodies were still dangling from the tree beside the smoking ruins of the whorehouse. They were cut down and buried in a potter's field. Next to their names in his jail register Sheriff Barclay wrote: "Taken out of jail by mob and lynched."

The town of Menominee, which had never before experienced a lynching, was in shock. Newspaper editor Luther B. Noyes wrote: "We have no words of commendation. On the contrary we have the most utter abhorrence and loathing for such barbaric deviltry as characterized by the lynching of the McDonalds."

Sheriff Barclay arrested Max Forvilly and several other ringleaders, but in the end nobody was ever convicted for the lynching. It was said, however, that some members of the vigilante mob died strange and violent deaths. One died in a fire, another died from a rattlesnake bite, a third drowned, and yet another was cut in two by a mill saw. Coincidence? Or did Father Heliard's prophecy come true?

6
GEORGE GARNETT AND THE UNION JACK BANDITS
Stagecoach Robbers

Stagecoach holdups were pretty rare in Canada. The command to "Stand and deliver" made famous by English highwaymen like Dick Turpin, or the gruff "Throw down the box" uttered by every American desperado from Jesse James to Black Bart, were seldom heard on the highways and byways of Canada. Even Bill Miner, the Gentleman Bandit who made a career between prison sentences out of robbing stagecoaches in the American West, didn't bother with them when he expanded his operations to Canada. He robbed trains instead. Ironically, the last stagecoach holdup in America's Old West period was pulled by a Canadian woman named Pearl Hart in 1899.

One of the reasons for the relative, compared to the American example. infrequency of robbery by road agents in the Canadian West was, of course, the presence of the North-West Mounted Police. In the American West a lawman's jurisdiction might end at a county or state line. North of the Forty-ninth Parallel the NWMP had no such obstacles. A constable could pursue a suspect, if not quite to the ends of the earth, then at least to the ends of the vast region once known as Rupert's Land.

As a result, though stagecoach travel across the Canadian prairies was just as dusty and bone-jarringly uncomfortable as it was on the American plains, the Canadian drivers and passengers were, for the most part, spared the unnerving experience of a holdup. Nevertheless, there were a few desperadoes who believed they could pull a quick stickup out on the lonely road and escape the long, red-sleeved arm of the law.

George F. Garnett of London, Ontario, went west with the Seventh Fusiliers in 1885 during the Riel Rebellion. He stayed in Winnipeg long enough to take a bride, then moved on to that part of the old Northwest Territories now called Saskatchewan. Garnett set himself up as a ferryman at the South Branch crossing of the Saskatchewan River, hauling passengers, livestock, and freight back and forth for a fee. River ferrymen in frontier regions at that time were notorious for being intemperate, profane, and unreliable. It was the kind of job taken by characters not generally suited for more conventional employment. George Garnett was the exception. He was a well-respected, church-going member of his community, and he operated his ferry as an efficient business and public service. George saw everyone safely across the river — farmers with produce, cowboys and their horses, Mounties on patrol.

Then, for some reason, this man who had never had any trouble with the law, and who was more likely to pick up a Bible than a gun, suddenly decided to take that wrong turn down the Old Outlaw Trail. He was still very much a newlywed, so perhaps he thought he needed the money to give himself a boost in his new life as a family man. Or maybe he had been reading too many of the dime novels and *Police Gazette* stories that made American outlaws legends in their own time.

Without a word of explanation to his wife or anyone else, Garnett arranged to have a hired man look after the ferry, and on July 12, 1886, he climbed into his wagon and set off for Salt Springs, an important stopover on the road between Prince Albert and Qu'Appelle. This was where passenger and mail coaches servicing the new Canadian Pacific Railway met. Everybody passed through here, and with them came their news. It didn't take Garnett long to gather just what he needed to know. A party of five men would be camping by the trail a few miles north of Salt Springs. The southbound stage from Prince Albert and the northbound stage from Qu'Appelle had rolled in on time and would undoubtedly depart on schedule in the morning. On the night of July 16, Garnett quietly rode out of town.

At three o'clock the next morning he surprised the five men camped by the trail north of Salt Springs. They had been drinking the night before, but according to one of them, Angus Thompson, they were awakened when a man shouted, "Bill, stand over to the other side of the tent." Then there was a gunshot, and a bullet whipped through the tent. The man called to them to crawl out on their hands and knees backwards. Four of them obeyed. When the fifth man didn't emerge, the stranger fired another shot through the tent. Thompson told him to stop shooting. The other man was drunk, he said, and couldn't hear a thing. Garnett told the hungover victims that a hidden gunman had them in his sights, so they better cooperate. He tied them up with bed cord and robbed them of $300, leaving them in a state of numbness but wondering nonetheless why he hadn't worn a mask.

With almost a working man's yearly wages in his pocket, Garnett turned his attention to the Prince Albert stagecoach. He hit it at about 1:00 p.m. Driver John Art was astonished to find himself facing an unmasked robber who was pointing a shotgun at him. Art thought the man was fooling until the bandit told him to get down or he would shoot. The driver's employer had instructed him to carry a revolver, but that day Art had left his gun at home. The only passengers, farmer Edward Fiddler and local politician John Betts, could hardly believe what was happening when the man ordered

In the early twentieth century, tourists pose for a "holdup" of the Seeing Saskatoon stage-coach. The coach pictured here is probably somewhat fancier than the one robbed by George Garnett in 1886. (Saskatchewan Archives Board R-A8218-2)

them out of the coach. One of them asked Garnett what he thought he was up to. "Get out quick, or I'll damn soon show you what I'm up to," he said, thumbing back the hammers on his shotgun. At the sound of the loud clicks the two men obeyed smartly.

The bandit made Art and Betts kneel and then tied their hands with bed cord. "I thought I could handle him, as I thought he had a shotgun," Art testified later. "But I turned my head a little and saw a revolver pointed at my back." The robber then ordered Fiddler to drive the coach behind a bluff while he and the two others walked behind.

"Where's the box?" Garnett asked when they were out of sight of the road. Art said he didn't know anything about any box. Garnett ransacked the stagecoach but couldn't find a strongbox. All he discovered was a bottle of whiskey. Frustrated, he tore into the mail bags and took the one with registered letters, the one most likely to contain money.

John Art complained that it wouldn't look good for him to have his stagecoach held up by just one man. Garnett told him not to worry. Another man was covering them with a gun at that very moment. In fact, Garnett went on, they had robbed a larger party that very morning. His man was just keeping out of sight. Garnett gave everybody a pull from the whiskey bottle, then searched the men. He found $250 on Betts but decided to let him keep it. It never hurt for a bandit to add a little Robin Hood touch. The registered mail Garnett had grabbed would yield over $1,000. With the money he had taken from the five men, that made for a pretty good day's haul, especially since he didn't have to split it with anyone. He said, "Now I'm done with you fellows," and walked away.

Garnett rode back to Salt Springs to get his wagon, then drove a hundred miles to Carrot River where he filed on a homestead. That was to be his alibi. Then he returned to South Branch, shaved off his beard and moustache, and resumed his job as ferrymen. The stolen money was buried nearby in a tin can.

The countryside was abuzz with talk of the stagecoach robbery. Even the *Globe* in distant Toronto reported on it. As was often the case, no one wanted to believe that a Canadian had been responsible for such an outrage. The robber, who was so bold he hadn't even worn a mask, must have been an American.

Then, about a month after the robbery, Garnett went to Prince Albert on business. Unfortunately for him, John Art was there. Art recognized the holdup man and informed the North-West Mounted Police. The Mounties arrested Garnett, who was subsequently identified by Art and some of the other robbery victims. He was sent to Regina to stand trial while the Mounties went looking for the loot. They tore apart Garnett's house and the ferryboat but found nothing. Garnett, protesting his innocence, pretended to know nothing about stolen money, even after clothing he had worn the day of the robbery was found on his property by the police and identified by Art.

However, Garnett *did* tell a man named Peter Smith, who shared a cell with him in the Regina jail. When Smith was released in September, he went straight to Garnett's cache and dug up the money. It would prove to be a very unlucky windfall for him.

Garnett went on trial for mail robbery in the first week of October. His attorney submitted as evidence an envelope he said had been mailed to him from Winnipeg. It contained some of the registered material that had been stolen from the stagecoach. The lawyer said the "real" robber had sent him the envelope because he didn't want an innocent man to go to jail. The jury didn't buy the story. Garnett was found guilty and sentenced to fourteen years in Stony Mountain Penitentiary. "I submit to the circumstances," he said upon being convicted. The Mounties were given a $250 reward for capturing the outlaw.

In prison the ever-devout Garnett served as assistant to the chaplain. After two years of exemplary behaviour, he walked out of jail dressed in clerical garb he had stolen from the chaplain and made his getaway with the reverend's horse and rig. He was soon recaptured and spent the next eight years behind bars. Garnett was eventually pardoned and then vanished from historical record.

For Peter Smith the booty from the robbery proved to be a ticket to doom. For several months after recovering the money, Smith went about his day-to-day life as the manager of a stagecoach stop on the Prince Albert trail. Then, in May 1887, he announced he was leaving. A few days later his body was found in the bush by the trail. Police suspected a Native boy named Nan-nan-kase-lex, who suddenly had plenty of money to spend. He claimed it was a gift from a Native woman who had befriended him. Police couldn't produce enough evidence to make a charge of murder stick. The Mounted Police had solved Saskatchewan's first stagecoach robbery, but not the subsequent murder of Peter Smith.

That same summer of 1886, hundreds of miles to the west, the territory that would soon be called Alberta was also treated to its first stagecoach holdup. On August 23 a driver named Braden left Calgary for the long run to Fort Edmonton. The round trip between towns took two weeks, and whether the experience was an adventure or an ordeal depended on one's own perspective. This time the passengers would have something to talk about besides cold river crossings, Spartan way stations, and whiskey-swilling drivers. About fifteen miles north of Calgary, driver Braden was confronted by two gunmen on horseback who ordered him to stop the coach. One of the bandits wore a mask of black cloth. The other's disguise was particularly distinctive. His mask was cut from a piece of the Union Jack! The outlaw might have been American or Irish; there were strong anti-British sentiments in both countries at that time. Whatever his reasons for desecrating the British flag, the robber gave himself and his partner a name — the Union Jack Bandits.

The road agents tore open the mail sacks and found nothing to interest them, so they robbed Braden and his passengers of whatever money and valuables they had on them. They ordered Braden to continue on to Fort Edmonton, then climbed onto their horses and rode west into the hills.

Hours later Superintendent William Antrobus of the Calgary NWMP post learned of the robbery. The descriptions passengers gave of the thieves matched those of two men wanted for questioning concerning an earlier robbery committed at Elbow River, southwest of Calgary. The superintendent was sure the same men were responsible for both crimes. He mounted a posse.

Spreading out from the scene of the crime, the searchers found a pair of overalls and a piece of a British flag partially hidden under a rock. One constable recognized the pants as those owned by John Young, a man who had recently served six months in jail on liquor charges. With no other leads Antrobus sent his seventeen constables and civilian volunteers across the countryside to look for tracks and to question homesteaders, ranchers, and Natives.

The possemen came up with only one tip. Someone had seen two strangers at the cabin of a man named Scott Krenger, known to neighbours as Clinker Scott. The Mounted Police were familiar with Clinker, but nobody seemed to know much about him. He claimed to be a prospector, but where his money actually came from was a mystery. When the Mounties questioned Clinker about the strangers, he said there had indeed been two men at his place. But they couldn't have been involved in the holdup, he said, because they had been at his cabin at the time of the robbery. Neither of them fitted the description of John Young.

Superintendent Antrobus had his men search Calgary high and low for Young without success. He didn't write off Clinker's visitors as suspects, nor, for that matter, Clinker himself. The Mountie's suspicions were well founded. A few days after the robbery the citizens of Calgary awoke to news of a murder.

A settler looking for a stolen wagon approached Clinker's cabin and was surprised to see no one around, though Clinker's horse was in the corral. Peering through the cabin window, the man saw Clinker Scott Krenger dead on the floor. He had been shot in the stomach. Clinker had apparently been taken by surprise while making biscuits, because his hands were covered with flour and a pan of dough was on the table. A medical examiner determined he had been murdered two days after the stagecoach robbery.

Had Clinker been involved with the mysterious Union Jack Bandits? Did they kill him in a quarrel over the loot? Or had he outlived his usefulness to them and been shot because the outlaws went by the old adage that dead men told no tales? The questions would remain unanswered. Despite an intense police search and painstaking work by plainclothes detectives, the Union Jack Bandits were never found. John Young was arrested in December 1886, but he had an alibi that police couldn't crack. The Union Jack Bandits, whoever they were, gave the lie to the myth that the Mounties "always got their man."

7
THE MOSES BROTHERS
Murder on Superior

*T*he Lake Superior country was wild and remote in the late nineteenth century. It was a rugged land of miners, timbermen, trappers, and railway men. It was also a land that saw frequent outbreaks of violence. According to a concerned editor of Port Arthur's *Weekly Herald and Algoma Miner,* "Life has been held to be cheap in this district, which has a record of many, many murders ..." The writer lamented the fact that few murders were successfully investigated, and when a suspect was brought to trial, a sympathetic jury inevitably let him go. The story of the Moses brothers of Heron Bay indicates that the editor had good cause for complaint.

Heron Bay, at the mouth of the Pic River, southeast of Marathon, was the home of the Pic Band of the Ojibwa Nation. For many years the people of the community lived in fear of the Moses brothers — Joseph, Mohawk, Louis, and Antoine. These men lived on their government annuity payments, by hunting and trapping, and by thievery when the opportunity presented itself. They were known to be prone to extreme violence when drinking. To make an enemy of one Moses brother was to make enemies of them all.

Sometime in the late 1880s the brothers were in the vicinity of Peninsular Harbour in the camp of their uncle, Antoine David, and his wife and children. As the bottle was being passed around, an argument flared up. Louis Moses seized a club, and while his brother Joe held a flaming torch for light, he bashed his uncle's head in, killing him on the spot.

David's son, William, a young man, fled into the bush, with Louis in pursuit. Louis overtook his cousin, battered him to the ground with the club, then pounded the youth's head to a pulp. He carried the dead man back to the camp, where his brothers helped him dispose of the bodies. Antoine David's wife and other children had witnessed the horrific events, and no doubt the Moses brothers warned them to keep their mouths shut. But David's daughter, eight years old at the time of the murders, would remember that terrible night some twelve years later.

Somehow word of the crimes reached authorities in Port Arthur. An inquest was held and warrants were issued for the arrest of the Moses brothers. They were never served. The outlaws retreated into the bush and stayed away from settlements for the next few years. According to the newspapers of the time, there were several more murders that went unsolved, including that of a fur trader who had been in possession of either money or a valuable load of pelts.

As time passed, the forces of law and order in Port Arthur forgot about Antoine and William David. Fear of the Moses brothers prevented anyone from reminding them. From all appearances the trouble had blown over. The brothers resumed collecting their annuity payments at Heron Bay.

Then, on a Sunday in July 1892, three Canadian Pacific Railway sectionmen, Thomas Mundon, Alex Cousineau, and Joseph Lemaise, along with Lemaise's twelve-year-old son, Dick, left Port Coldwell in a sailboat for Pie Island, about twelve miles from Port Arthur. Living in a summer camp on the island were the Moses brothers and their sisters, Mary Anne, Catharine, and Susan. The girls evidently were teenagers.

When the white men arrived at the camp, Louis and Joe were off in the bush. The sectionmen had whiskey, which they shared with all of the Natives present except the youngest, Mary Anne. Soon Catharine and Susan were "pretty well on," as Mary Anne would put it later.

At some point Lemaise got up and left the wigwam in which they had all been drinking. He had two half bottles of whiskey and headed off into the bush, apparently looking for Louis and Joe. Mary Anne would testify that inside the wigwam one of the white men was lying on the ground with Catharine. His arm was around her and he was tickling her. Susan and the other white man were sitting and talking. She didn't say what Mohawk and Antoine were doing, nor whether young Dick was in the wigwam.

Suddenly, there was a gunshot! All of the Natives ran out to investigate, but Mundon and Cousineau remained inside. Mary Anne was about fifty feet behind the wigwam when she heard two more shots come from that direction. When she looked back, she saw Louis and Joe drag out the bodies of the two white men. The brothers went into the bush and returned with the body of Lemaise. They rifled through the pockets of the murdered men and found only $5 and Mundon's silver watch.

With Dick Lemaise looking on in shock and terror, the four Moses brothers tied large stones to the bodies and placed them in the sailboat. They climbed into the boat and took it out a way, then tipped it over. As the bodies sank, the brothers swam back to shore. Anyone finding the overturned boat would assume the three men had met with an accident and drowned.

Now there was the problem of what to do about Dick. A few years earlier Louis had murdered his own uncle and cousin. It seemed he was capable of anything. But perhaps others in the family interceded on the youngster's behalf. Mary Anne, after all, was probably not much older than the boy. Whatever happened, when the Moses brothers went back into the bush on the mainland, they took the white boy with them.

For almost six years people along the North Superior shore believed the missing men and boy had drowned when their boat capsized on the lake. Nonetheless, Louis and Joe kept to the woods, emerging only to collect their annuities at Heron Bay. They established what was described as a "fortified camp" at the junction of the Black and Pic rivers. As time passed, it seemed that once again they would get away with murder.

In the spring of 1898, however, rumours began to circulate of evil doings on Pie Island. The missing sectionmen, people whispered, hadn't drowned but had been robbed and murdered by the Moses brothers. Furthermore, the young son of one of the dead men had been carried off into the woods, never to be seen again. Louis Moses, the story claimed, had murdered him.

On June 17, John Desmoulin, Joseph Goodchild, and their wives were going down the Pic River on a timber raft. As they neared the Moses brothers' camp, four shots rang out from the shore, one of the bullets striking a skiff being towed behind the raft. Desmoulin and Goodchild went ashore, and showing no fear of Louis Moses, demanded to know why he had shot at them. Louis said the shooting had been accidental, but it was later surmised that he had thought Goodchild knew something about the death of Dick Lemaise.

The stories of murders and shootings eventually reached the ears of authorities in Port Arthur. J.F. Hodder, the Department of Indians Affairs agent there, corresponded with Ottawa. Apparently, the suspected murder of white men was a much more serious matter than the suspected murder of Natives. An order was issued for the Moses brothers' arrest.

The police didn't attempt an assault on the Moses brothers' camp. The outlaws would almost certainly put up a fight, resulting in further injury and death. Moreover, if any of the brothers escaped into the woods, potential witnesses would be afraid to give evidence. Instead, the police quietly planned an ambush in the one place where they could be sure to catch all four brothers together.

Monday, July 18, was the day the members of the Pic Band collected their annuity payments. To do so they had to go to an office in Heron Bay. When the unsuspecting Moses brothers showed up, they were met by Agent Hodder, his clerk W.H. Arnold, and three provincial police constables named Whalen, Conner, and Dodd, all of whom were armed. The Natives hadn't brought their guns with them, but they still put up a struggle. The officers managed to subdue the four and handcuff them without shooting anyone. One of the brothers was found to be in possession of Mundon's silver watch.

The police hustled the prisoners onto a train to Port Arthur. One of the brothers —accounts don't say who — tried to escape by jumping from the train when it had to reduce speed, but was quickly recaptured. They were lodged in the Port Arthur jail pending trial.

At a hearing held in early August the brothers — all described in the press as handsome men — heard their own sisters tell the court what had happened on Pie Island. They also listened while the daughter of Antoine David, now twenty years old, told what Louis and Joe had done to her father and brother. Everything had to be said through an interpreter, because none of the brothers spoke English.

At the end of the hearing Louis and Joe confessed that what their sisters had said was true. They took full responsibility for killing Thomas Munden, Alex Cousineau, and Joseph Lemaise. Antoine and Mohawk, they said, had nothing to do with the murders. Their only part had been in helping to dump the bodies in the lake.

They denied killing Dick Lemaise. The brothers said they had taken the boy into the bush with them and kept him for two years. They claimed he had drowned when a canoe overturned in rapids. This story did nothing to quell the rumour that Louis had murdered the boy to silence him. Aside from young Miss David's testimony, little was said regarding the David murders.

The case went to trial before Chief Justice Armour in early December. The brothers were being tried only for the murder of Cousineau. What happened in the Port Arthur courtroom was, to say the least, peculiar.

The magistrate heard Mary Anne Moses retell her story about what had happened on Pie Island — the story her brothers had already admitted was true. Then the defence argued that the motive for the killings wasn't robbery, as everyone had initially assumed. Mr. McWatt, the Moses brothers' lawyer, said his clients had been

Port Arthur celebrates Queen Victoria's Jubilee in 1897. One year later the Moses brothers were brought here to stand trial for murder. (Thunder Bay Public Library Archives P458)

outraged that the three deceased men had been seducing their young sisters with liquor, and that the brothers themselves were under the influence when they killed the white men. There was a pause in the proceedings then as McWatt conferred with his clients and both McWatt and the Crown prosecutor conferred with Judge Armour. It was decided that Louis and Joe Moses would plead guilty to a reduced charge of manslaughter, for which they would be sentenced to ten years in Kingston Penitentiary. Mohawk and Antoine, who hadn't actually killed anyone, though they had helped to cover up two multiple murders and had participated in an abduction, were released on probation. The judge gave them a stern warning about the evils of alcohol. All other charges were dropped!

Then Judge Armour launched into a tirade in which he denounced white men like Munden, Cousineau, and Lemaise, who debauched Native women with liquor. That crime, he implied, was almost as bad as the crime of homicide with which the prisoners had been charged. As Port Arthur's *Herald* reported, "He could not find language sufficiently strong to express how he felt about such a state of affairs. Oh, but he did roast the characters under review."

It may well have been that the slain men had been plying the Moses girls with liquor, but those men weren't there in court to argue the charge. The Moses brothers had seen to that by taking the law into their own hands when they might just as easily have sent the offenders packing. And what about the murders of Antoine and William David? The editor of the *Herald* asked that question. But with the Moses brothers' reign of terror finally brought to an end, it seemed nobody saw any need to answer it.

8 THE NAPANEE BANK HEIST
An Inside Job?

*N*orth American bank robbers of the late nineteenth and early twentieth centuries were fond of saying, "It's easy to stick up a bank. It's the getaway that's hard." Walking into a bank with drawn guns and demanding money required a reckless kind of nerve and posed a number of dangers to men out for "easy money." For one thing, there were always witnesses involved, and masks and disguises were never a hundred percent effective. Also, unlike today's bank employees, the managers and tellers of that era, almost all of them male, were *expected* to do whatever they could to protect the bank's assets. There was usually a gun in the manager's office, and sometimes in the tellers' drawers, too. If the opportunity arose during a holdup, the bank employee was supposed to do the manly thing. For the bandits this meant not only the possibility of getting wounded or killed themselves but of leaving behind dead victims, with the subsequent charge of murder hanging over them. The other big disadvantage to armed robbery was that once the outlaw got out of the bank with the swag, there was almost immediate pursuit by the police.

For these reasons many criminals opted for the less-dramatic but also less-dangerous method of bank burglary. In a well-planned burglary there were few witnesses, if any. There wasn't much chance of a shootout, though some bank burglars carried guns in case of discovery. Best of all, the bandits could be miles from the scene of the crime by the time the robbery was discovered.

The biggest problem for a bank burglar lay in getting at the loot, which was always locked in a safe or a vault, sometimes both, inside a securely locked bank. The less-talented thieves would gain entry to the bank by means of an axe or a crowbar and then use whatever force was necessary, even explosives, to open the safe. But such methods were noisy and apt to attract attention. The elite among the bank burglars were the "cracksmen," those experts who had made a study of locks of all types and could quietly make a vault or safe surrender its treasure. The very best setup occurred when the robber gang had a man on the "inside" — a dishonest bank employee who, for a share of the booty, would pass on vital information such as the combination to a lock. The pistol-packin' stickup men, whose exploits inspired the writers of dime novels and *Police Gazette* stories, might have been scornful of these shadowy men and their cautious ways, but to bank managers they were the bogeymen of bad dreams.

Such a nightmare awaited manager H.H. Baines of the Dominion Bank of Napanee, Ontario, on the morning of Saturday, August 28, 1897. To his surprise he found he couldn't open the vault. The combination had been mysteriously changed. Teller William Hamilton Ponton remarked that they would be in a fix if they couldn't get the vault open. Baines arranged to borrow some cash from another bank in town and sent for a locksmith. Not until Saturday evening was the vault door finally opened, Baines thinking all the while that something was wrong with the mechanism of the lock. Then he discovered he couldn't open the safe, either. A feeling of dread came over the manager as the locksmith went to work on the safe. When the door was finally opened, Baines realized the awful truth — $32,000 in gold and silver coins and banknotes was missing. Gone, too, was his own private collection of rare coins. News of the robbery shook the little town of Napanee, just east of Kingston, and made front-page headlines in Toronto and across the country. It would hold public attention for many months to come as one of the most sensational bank burglary cases in the history of Canadian crime.

The clues left at the scene of the crime were baffling. Holes had been bored in the wall of a woodshed at the back of the bank, and the robbers had evidently used the shed as cover while gaining entry to the building. The janitor told police that for some time prior to the robbery there had been screens hanging against the wall, hiding the holes from view. Sometimes there were bicycles leaning against the screens. Ponton and another teller named Durand rode bicycles. The burglars had evidently had little trouble opening the bank's vault. The combination of the vault was known to Baines, Ponton, Durand, and junior clerk W.H. Greene. The safe within the vault had a more difficult lock, the combination of which was known only to Baines and Durand. The thieves had drilled holes into the side of the iron safe but had been stymied by a plate of impenetrable cold steel. The useless holes had been covered over with grease and soot and weren't discovered until police examined the safe. The thieves had subsequently figured out the combination of the safe, an accomplishment police said would have taken many weeks of study by trial and error. Inside the safe, Baines, Ponton, Durand, and Greene each had his own compartment. All had been forced open and cleaned out.

For two months prior to the robbery, two, sometimes four, tramps had been camped at a spot on the banks of the Napanee River just a couple of miles out of town. They had often been seen loitering around town after sunset. Two weeks before the big burglary the home of a local resident was broken into. Edward Sills, high constable of Lennox and Addington County, apprehended two of the tramps as suspects. He had no evidence to hold them, and after keeping them in jail for a night, he told them to get out of town. One of them had in his pocket a roll of pennies such as might be found in a bank teller's drawer. Sills didn't think anything of it at the time, because no one had reported any theft of rolled coins. The tramps seemingly kept out of Napanee, as ordered, but continued to hang around their riverside camp. They were gone the very day the robbery was discovered.

This was too big a case for ordinary county constables to handle. From Toronto came veteran provincial government detective William Greer and Dominion Bank inspector Clarence Bogart. To assist the Canadian officers, some would say actually to dominate the investigation, two Pinkerton detectives travelled up from New York City — George Dougherty and a man named Wilkes. Canadian banks belonged to the Bankers Association of North America, a client of the Pinkerton Detective Agency, so there was nothing illegal about the American sleuths being involved in the investigation.

The police were certain the vanished tramps had something to do with the robbery, and they were just as convinced the burglars had been given help. The robbery had all the marks of an inside job, and suspicion soon fell on William Ponton.

Twenty-five-year-old Billy Ponton was a native of Belleville and a man of solid reputation. He was very popular around town and had never been in trouble with the law in his life. He was said to be "well connected." His cousin, Colonel W.H. Ponton, was a highly respected military man.

Nonetheless, some of young Ponton's activities aroused police suspicions. Prior to the robbery he had moved from his old lodgings across the street from the bank to a boarding house with a backyard that bordered the ground behind the bank. His room was on the second floor and at the rear of the house. Below his window was a shed by which a person could easily climb down to the ground.

Ponton wasn't married, and from all appearances he lived modestly on his income of about $500 a year from the bank. He wasn't known for any sort of immoral behaviour, though he took an occasional drink and admitted to playing penny-ante poker with the other lads at the bank. But right after the robbery he took care of a clothing bill and paid the balance he owed on his bicycle. When police interviewed him, he had $80 in cash on him, a large sum for a man of such modest means.

Ponton claimed he had paid the bills out of his savings and from money he had received from a small accident insurance policy. When the police learned he didn't have a savings account at the very bank at which he was employed, he explained he didn't want his employer to know he had accumulated a nest egg on his humble salary. Ponton also complained it was "impertinent" of the police to inquire into his personal finances.

Asked to account for himself on the night of the robbery, Ponton said he had been in the company of friends until about 10:30 p.m. He had returned to his room alone, he said, and gone to bed at midnight. Ponton insisted he had stayed there until eight the following morning when he got up to go to work. But a Mrs. McGreer, who occupied the room above Ponton's, said that on that very night she had heard movements and men's voices coming from below at a very late hour. Ponton denied there had been anybody else in his room and became indignant when Dougherty suggested he had sneaked a woman in that night.

The police weren't satisfied with Ponton's explanations and arrested him on suspicion of robbery. Then Dougherty spent almost three hours searching Ponton's room. He didn't find any money, but he did produce a piece of office paper from the bank with a drawing of a key on it. He said it matched the key for the door of the bank and could have been used to make a duplicate. The news hit the papers, and Napanee was electrified.

A preliminary hearing was scheduled for October, and as the time approached it became obvious that almost the entire town was on Ponton's side. Anyone who chose to believe the young clerk was guilty was well advised to keep his opinion to himself. People didn't take it well when it was reported that Dougherty said Ponton had "a shifty manner." An editor at Toronto's *Globe* called it "harsh and cruel" that Ponton's mother wasn't allowed to visit him in jail without a police officer present. There were rumours that police were "sweating" the prisoner — that is, subjecting him to intense questioning accompanied by physical and verbal abuse. Both Ponton and the police denied this had happened, but the young man's sympathizers weren't convinced. No one trusted the American Pinkerton men, and there was a general feeling of hostility towards them.

The Crown's case against Ponton was flimsy. No one had witnessed him outside his room the night of the robbery. No one had ever spotted him in the company of the mysterious tramps. He denied he had ever seen the drawing of the key before it was produced in court. A rumour circulated that the Pinkerton men had "planted" the drawing in an attempt to get a conviction and make themselves look good. A lock expert testified that it would have been impossible to make a duplicate key from the drawing.

When the judge announced there wasn't enough evidence to hold Ponton for trial and that he was free to go, a great cheer arose from the capacity crowd in the courtroom and from the throng waiting in the street outside. Ponton was carried through Napanee in a torchlight parade, and a brass band played "A Hot Time in

Our Town Tonight." Ponton and his lawyer, E. Gus Porter, were called on to make speeches, and somebody cried, "Three cheers for Billy Ponton's mother!"

The Pinkerton men, meanwhile, kept out of sight. There had been angry cries that they should be pelted with rotten eggs, tarred and feathered, and run out of town. Some bank clerks in Kingston had sent a case of old eggs marked "Vintage 1876" just for the occasion. But the crowd dispersed without doing anyone harm. Greer, Bogart, and the Pinkerton men quietly continued with their investigation.

Early in 1898 Ponton filed a lawsuit against the Dominion Bank, seeking $40,000 in damages for, among other things, false arrest and defamation of character. The case was delayed as the bank's lawyers fought to have the venue changed to Belleville. They said the bank would never get a fair hearing in Napanee, where there was so much hard feeling against it. The citizens there, Toronto's *Evening Star* reported, were behind Ponton "all the way." This legal jousting was still going on in July when the break came that the police had been awaiting for almost a year. Some of the stolen money was circulating in Montreal.

Part of the loot taken the previous August had been $10,000 in unsigned $10 bills. At that time many banks issued their own currency. Before a bill could be put into circulation it had to be signed by the manager of the bank branch from which it was issued. Otherwise it was worthless. The bills that had surfaced in Montreal bore the forged signature of H.H. Baines. Montreal police soon had a woman named Caroline Saucier in custody. From her they got information that led them to thirty-five-year-old Robert Mackie of Belleville and fifty-three-year-old George Edward Pare, Saucier's brother, who was hiding out in Manchester, New Hampshire. Police there found that Pare had been passing off the Canadian bills with the forged signatures in their community, too.

Because Ponton and Mackie were both natives of Belleville, the police tried to establish a connection between them. Ponton admitted he was acquainted with Mackie, as he was with most of the people in the small town. But he denied they were friends. Mackie was known around town as a "sport," and he and Ponton didn't move in the same social circles. Some of the rare coins from the collection stolen from the Napanee safe were found in Mackie's home.

Baines identified them as his, though Mackie's wife said her husband had had them for years.

George Pare was a Montreal-born criminal who spoke English with a thick French Canadian accent. He was a slender, sickly man who had done prison time in both Canada and the United States. At the time of his arrest for the Napanee job he was wanted by Quebec police for another robbery in Montreal. He was known in the Montreal underworld as an expert "cracksman." A large part of the swag from the Napanee burglary was found in a secret compartment in a box in his Manchester residence. Pare was an old hand at the real-life game of cops and robbers and knew he had been nailed with the goods. He didn't relish the idea of another long stretch in prison, so in return for the promise of a light sentence, he agreed to sell out his partners. Pare sent the police to the Boston hideout of another Montrealer, fifty-six-year-old William Henry Holden.

When police burst into Holden's apartment, Holden's wife and eleven-year-old daughter began tossing bundles of Canadian money into the stove while he struggled with the officers. He was a big, strong man and was difficult to subdue. But the police got him handcuffed and rescued the money before it could be burnt up. It was easily identified as part of the haul from the Napanee bank.

William Holden had served two prison terms in Canada for robberies and had been in trouble for breaking jail and for beating up a policeman. He didn't consider the latter offences crimes at all. Holden blamed the police for his troubles. He said he had tried to go straight after his second stint behind bars, but that every time he got an honest job, detectives informed his employer that he was a jailbird, resulting in his dismissal. How, he wanted to know, was a man supposed to support a wife and four children with the police hounding him? He swore he would get even with Pare for ratting on him.

Ponton said he was overjoyed to hear of the arrests. He told the press, "Now people will know who really robbed the bank." But stool pigeon Pare hadn't finished talking. He implicated an Ontario crook named John Roach, whereabouts unknown. And he said the original idea to rob the bank had come from a clerk — Billy Ponton!

By now the attention of the whole nation was on the little Ontario town, and the news travelled like a shockwave from Halifax to Victoria. But in Napanee the Pontonites, as they were now called, refused to abandon their hero. While a few of the male citizens shook their heads in silent disgust with themselves for having believed in Ponton's innocence, the majority brandished their fists and declared Pare a liar who would drag down an innocent man to secure his own freedom. Pare was, by his own admission, a criminal with a sordid career going back thirty years. He had said with pride that he never regretted committing a robbery, only getting caught. Who could believe such a villain? The women of Napanee especially rallied to the cause of the handsome young bank clerk, and it was they who would occupy most of the courtroom seats in the series of trials about to get underway.

Ponton was arrested again. Because his first hearing had only been held to determine if there was enough evidence to go to trial, he couldn't seek the shelter of the law that forbade the state to try a person for the same crime twice. Ponton said he wanted a trial to clear his name once and for all. He again called upon E. Gus Porter to defend him, and the lawyer secured his release on bail.

According to the story Pare told police, Ponton approached Mackie with the idea of robbing the bank. The clerk allegedly said he would know when there was a lot of money in the safe and that he could help the burglars get into the bank and give them the combination for the vault. But he didn't know the combination for the safe. Mackie contacted Holden in Montreal. John T. Roach was also brought into the scheme. According to Pare, over a dozen people were involved, from the ones who would actually make the heist to those who would help circulate the stolen money.

William H. Ponton, William Holden, and George Edward Pare — the principal suspects of the Napanee bank heist. (Toronto *Globe*)

Holden allegedly met Ponton in his room. The clerk provided a key with which the burglars could enter the back door of the bank, and the combination for the vault. The holes found drilled in the back wall from under the cover of the woodshed were put there to confound the police.

With Mackie posted as lookout, Holden and Roach entered the bank several times. On one occasion they had to leave in a hurry because a night watchman was out front. They tried unsuccessfully to drill the safe. Roach suggested they send for expert help — George Pare.

Pare, as he told the story, cast himself as the skilled veteran who came to the aid of incompetents. In their hobo camp by the river, Roach, Pare, Holden, and Mackie discussed various ways of getting at the "boodle." One suggestion was to waylay Durand as he rode his bicycle and force him to give up the combination of the safe. Pare dismissed that as amateurish. Another idea was to have Ponton go to the bank one evening and get the other clerks engaged in a poker game. Then Holden, Pare, Mackie, and Roach could burst in with guns drawn, bind and gag everybody, including Ponton, and force Durand to open the safe. They went so far as to get some rope and cloth to make gags and masks, which police later found in a hiding place. But even though Pare and Holden had guns, Pare finally turned down the plan. He was, he said, a coward at heart and wouldn't go along with any plan in which he might get hurt. Roach finally grew weary of the inaction and departed for greener pastures, but with the understanding that if the others succeeded in pulling off the job, he would get a share for his time and trouble.

Pare said he came to the conclusion that the only way to get into the safe was for him to crack it. This required numerous late-night visits to the bank during which he carefully studied the lock and worked on it, never leaving any telltale signs. It was during one of these secret visitations that Holden had scooped some rolls of pennies from a teller's drawer so they could buy food. No one reported the missing rolls of coins.

Ponton, said Pare, kept them informed of the amount of money in the bank from day to day and told them he believed there was $10,000 in negotiable bonds in the safe. The clerk hadn't actually seen the bonds but had seen references to them in Mr. Baines's paperwork. Mackie said he knew a shady lawyer in Belleville who could help them dispose of the bonds. (As it turned out, the bonds were actually in the bank's head office in Toronto, but investigators would wonder how Pare knew about them at all.) Pare said that at one point Holden wanted out of the scheme, but that Ponton said he himself would stick with it all the way.

After Constable Sills ordered them out of town, Pare continued, he and Holden knew they would have to make their move before they were chased out of the county altogether or jailed as vagrants. He finally worked out the safe's combination. Then he told Ponton to get Baines to sign as many of the $10 bills as he could without arousing the manager's suspicion. Ponton, he said, later told him he had done that.

On the night of the robbery, Pare continued, he had gone with Holden and Mackie to Ponton's room. Late at night the three of them climbed out the window and crossed the yard to the bank. Mackie, as usual, stood guard while the other two went inside. Opening the safe, Pare boasted, was easy. The key to Ponton's compartment was in his teller's drawer. Inside was Ponton's share of the loot, $5,000, already neatly wrapped in a package. The other compartments had to be jimmied open. Just to make things look good, the robbers smashed the lock on Ponton's compartment. They buried their burglar tools in the earth floor of the woodshed, where police later found them.

It was about 1:00 a.m. when they returned to Ponton's room through the window, Pare said. Ponton hung a blanket over the window so no light would show through, then he lit a lamp and they all sat at a table to divide the money. A cut of $1,000 was set aside for Roach, and Pare said that at some point he did give the man his money.

When the spoils were divided, Pare said he wouldn't let Ponton have his share right away. He was afraid the young clerk would draw suspicion to himself. Pare gave him $125 and told him he and Holden would bury the rest and return in a few months to give it to him when things cooled down. Ponton reluctantly agreed. Then the three bandits left the boarding house. Mackie went home to Belleville. Holden and Pare buried Ponton's money beside the railway track. They walked to Kingston, caught the first train to Montreal, and there parted company, agreeing to meet again in April.

Pare said he had been on his way to Detroit "on business" when he heard about Ponton's court hearing. He stopped in Napanee to see how things turned out. Pare said he had watched from the shadows as the town celebrated Ponton's release.

In April, he continued, he and Holden met Ponton in Belleville and gave him his share of the money. Pare said they "fined" the clerk a few hundred dollars because they believed that while the money was being divided in his room, Ponton had sneakily pocketed a few $50 bills.

At the hearings that began in August 1898, and at the trial that started in November, Pare repeated his story under oath. When Holden took the stand he, too, said Ponton was in on the job. Much of what he said supported Pare's testimony, but Gus Porter found a few discrepancies to pounce on.

Mackie said the whole story was a lie, that he was only casually acquainted with Ponton and didn't know Pare and Holden at all. But many witnesses identified Pare and Holden as the tramps who had been camped by the river, and some said they had seen Mackie with them. Mackie's own cousin testified that she had seen tools that looked like burglar's equipment in his room.

Nobody, though, had ever seen Ponton with the two confessed bank robbers. Pare had given the court an accurate description of Ponton's room, but Porter said he could have gotten that information from someone else, or could even have looked into the room from the roof of the shed beneath the window. Pare and Holden, Porter charged, were lying in return for leniency. Both criminals, he said, were being coached on what to say by the Pinkerton men, Dougherty and Wilkes, who had returned to Napanee for the trial. Would anyone who had just participated in a robbery, he asked, be foolish enough to entrust such men with $5,000?

The prosecution insisted that Pare and Holden must have had inside help to open the vault. Porter brought in lock experts who demonstrated for the jury that a skilled "cracksman," if given enough time, could open any lock. Pare had certainly had plenty of time and had shown his know-how with locks by changing the combinations on the vault and safe to delay the discovery of the crime.

Porter brought in clergymen, teachers, policemen, and Colonel W.H. Ponton as character witnesses for his client. He had a letter from a convict currently serving a sentence in Kingston who had once been in jail with Pare. The convict said Pare was a born liar. Former Montreal police chief Michael Cullen shared that opinion. He told the court that twelve years earlier when Pare was an inmate in St. Vincent de Paul Penitentiary the man had tried to get time taken off his sentence by implicating a respectable Montreal banker in a robbery plot. The "information" he had volunteered turned out to be a pack of lies. The retired policeman said he had no doubt the shifty little crook was up to the same trick with Ponton.

Constable Sills was overheard saying that by the time the trial was over, Ponton "will need a coffin instead of a brass band." But the women of Napanee were still solidly in the handsome bachelor's camp. They sent him bouquets of flowers and packed the courtroom day after day. On one August afternoon Toronto's *Globe* reported that of the 150 seats in the gallery, 144 were occupied by women.

At the conclusion of the first trial on December 7, Mackie was found guilty and sentenced to ten years in Kingston Penitentiary. The jury couldn't reach a unanimous decision on the charges against Ponton, and a new trial was scheduled for spring. Disappointment that Ponton hadn't been freed turned to anger, and a mob took to the streets of Napanee. The judge had to be escorted from the courthouse by a phalanx of policemen while angry citizens hurled insults at him. Not until the sheriff read the Riot Act did the crowd disperse. It was later learned that ten of the jurymen had voted for Ponton's acquittal, but two had stubbornly insisted he was guilty. Fortunately for the two, their names weren't made public.

Ponton spent the winter months still out on bail, while Pare and Holden remained in jail. There had been some concern when they were first arrested that some of their underworld cronies would try to spring them. But as the months passed and no such attempt was made, police vigilance began to slacken. For "economic reasons," as one newspaper put it, the two prisoners were alone in the jail at night. It wasn't the sort of opportunity a man of Pare's talents could pass up. He was just waiting for warm weather.

April came and arrangements were being made to move the venue elsewhere, since officials didn't believe an impartial trial could be held in Napanee. Then, on the morning of May 2, the turnkey of the county jail entered the building and found that his two star boarders were gone. Pare had removed bricks from the wall separating his cell from the one next door, which was unoccupied and not locked. He had then picked the lock on Holden's cell. The two had used a rope made from blankets to get over the jail yard wall.

Detective Greer traced the fugitives to a hobo camp near the town of Coteau, but from there the trail disappeared. It was generally believed they fled to the United States. "Pare and Holden will never be caught," a Toronto police inspector predicted.

Ponton expressed disgust when he learned of the escape. "I was anxious for the trial to come off this spring," he told the press. "I am sick of having such charges hanging over me, and now this escape, I suppose, throws it back further than ever."

While Ponton fumed impatiently over this latest disappointment, police sent pictures of the wanted men to cities across Canada and the United States. A reward of $1,000 was posted for their capture. Not until the first week of July did police get word, to their surprise, that the fugitives were still in Canada. They had travelled by freight train to Campbellton, New Brunswick, and were spotted playing dice in a saloon there by R. St. Onge, a sharp-eyed bank manager. He had carefully studied the photographs of the two bank robbers and had no doubt of their identities. Holden had evidently forgotten all about his oath to get even with Pare for turning him in. Maybe he simply realized he wasn't clever enough to get very far on his own as a fugitive.

The two almost managed to slip away again. St. Onge had a difficult time convincing the local constables that two of the most wanted men in Canada were right under their noses. The small-town coppers thought it unlikely that the notorious duo would show up in their little community. When Pare and Holden realized they had been recognized, they made a run for it. St. Onge, who was as big a man as Holden, tackled him as he tried to climb a fence and brought him down. The constables easily collared the scrawny Pare.

Detective Greer took the train to New Brunswick and escorted the escapees back to Napanee. Holden was sullen over this most recent loss of freedom, but in his cell Pare cheerfully regaled newspapermen with stories about his "little vacation." He gave a very low rating indeed to the accommodations of the Campbellton jail.

The recapture of Holden and Pare wasn't the only good news the police had in that summer of 1899. John Roach was arrested in Boston and was being held there until Canadian police could fetch him. High Constable Sills did the honours while Greer was in New Brunswick. Roach, a native of St. Thomas, Ontario, was yet another career criminal who had served time behind bars. He boasted that his specialty wasn't robbing banks but picking pockets. Roach said he had plied his trade in American cities from Chicago to Boston because "Canada was no good."

The new trial got underway in Cobourg in September. The courtroom was in a basement, with wood shavings on the floor for the benefit of tobacco chewers. When Roach took the stand, he, too, said Ponton had been in on the robbery. He claimed he himself had never received his promised share of the money, though Pare had testified that he had. "I wouldn't trust Pare's right hand to give money to his left," Roach said. He testified he had quit the gang because he got tired of waiting for the others to make up their minds about the job. Roach also said he was growing weary of Pare, who "wanted to be general."

E. Gus Porter hammered away on the point of William Ponton being a man of spotless reputation who had never had an iota of trouble with the law, while Pare, Holden, and Roach were all lifelong thieves and liars. The lawyer produced witnesses who gave alibis for Ponton for the time that Pare and Holden claimed he was in Belleville collecting his share of the loot. H.H. Baines testified he did, in fact, sign a lot of $10 bills just before the robbery, but that Ponton hadn't asked him to do so. The three known criminals, said Porter, could have dragged the names of *any* of the bank's employees into their craftily woven story, even that of Mr. Baines himself. But they had seen Ponton's name in the newspapers during that first investigation after the robbery and had invented a yarn in case they were caught.

Public interest in the case was starting to decline after it had been front-page news for so long; it was now competing for headline space with the Boer War. But it was still said that to express an opinion against Ponton was to invite a punch in the nose or a drop of poison in your whiskey or beer. A Cobourg waitress told a reporter from Toronto's *Evening Star*, "You're no good in this town unless you're for Ponton."

By September 23 all the evidence was in and the jury retired to deliberate. It took them only an hour to find Billy Ponton not guilty. Once again the young man was paraded through the streets in triumph while a brass band played "For He's a Jolly Good Fellow." He told the cheering crowd, "I was never nervous through the trial."

George Pare, who had informed on his friends and turned Queen's evidence but then had broken out of jail, was sentenced to three years in Kingston Penitentiary. The weaselly little safecracker, who one reporter described as "a viper by disposition," considered the outcome a victory of sorts; under the circumstances he might have been sent away for ten or twenty years.

William Holden and John Roach were also treated with leniency because they had testified for the Crown. Holden got four years, and the unbelievably lucky Roach was released under a suspended sentence. In December two American hoodlums arrested in Detroit were found to be in possession of hundreds of dollars in unsigned Canadian $10 bills from the Napanee robbery. No doubt those men had connections with Pare.

William Ponton didn't press his lawsuit against the Dominion Bank. He took a job as a cigar salesman. The teller was cleared of all charges because the only evidence against him had been the words of three notorious felons. His peers almost unanimously believed in his innocence. But there must have been a few people who looked at the former bank clerk with the boyishly handsome face and wondered if for just once in his life George Edward Pare had been telling the truth.

9
GEORGE O'BRIEN
Murder on a Yukon Trail

A nineteenth-century gold rush, whether it was across the continent to California, into the Native American country of the Black Hills of Dakota, or into the frigid Arctic wilderness of the Yukon, was a magnet for people of all stripes. There were the miners, most of them amateurs, who would break their backs panning the streams and shovelling the muck in search of the elusive yellow. Then there were the camp followers, the ones who, more often than not, were the people who really profited from the gold rush. These included the legitimate merchants who grubstaked the prospectors and sold them everything from flour and whiskey to picks and shovels — at inflated prices. Close behind the merchants were the conmen, gamblers, and prostitutes who were ever ready to relieve a man of his "poke" in return for a few minutes' pleasure or an opportunity to double or triple his fortune. Finally, there were those men who preyed on all of the others and sought their mother-lode at the point of a gun.

When word of Klondike gold echoed around the world in the autumn of 1896, the North-West Mounted Police was determined that Canadian territory wouldn't witness the kind of anarchy that had prevailed in the gold camps of California and American boom-towns like Deadwood and Tombstone. The Mounties quickly set up police posts in the gold-rush country and established the rule of law in Dawson City, the Mecca for thousands of stampeders heading for the Yukon. The boys could "whoop it up," in the immortal words of Robert W. Service, but there were no Dangerous Dan McGrew shootouts. The men were forbidden to carry guns in town.

The great majority of the gold seekers were Americans, and many of them objected to what they considered British Redcoat tyranny. But the Mounties had only to point across the border to Skagway, Alaska, as a grim reminder of what might happen in Dawson City in their absence. Skagway, the principal port on the route to the gold fields, was ruled by crime boss Jefferson Randolph "Soapy" Smith and was a cesspool of murder, robbery, fraud, and corruption. The Mounties were particularly vigilant about keeping Soapy Smith's riffraff out of the Yukon.

Nonetheless, with hordes of starry-eyed adventurers swarming along the Yukon trails, it was impossible to screen out all of the ne'er-do-wells. Those who ran afoul of the law might be banished to the American side of the line or fined. For those who couldn't pay their fines, there was the option of a few days, weeks, or months in a Mountie jail. Prisoners didn't spend their days lounging on a cot in the comfort of a warm cell. It took a lot of firewood to keep the Yukon cold at bay, so convicted men were kept busy chopping fuel for the Mounties' woodpile.

One man who spent a few months on the woodpile in 1899 was George O'Brien, an Englishman who had done time in Britain's Dartmoor Prison. He had gone to the Yukon in search of riches, but if he ever swished a pan in an icy stream or drove a pick into iron-hard permafrost, he soon gave it up in favour of a less-strenuous pursuit — robbery. O'Brien was jailed for pilfering from caches, stores of food set aside by miners and trappers. Such thievery wasn't done strictly for subsistence. Businessmen in Dawson and the operators of roadhouses along the trails between settlements were often willing to buy canned food and staples like flour, no questions asked. O'Brien made one attempt to escape custody but was recaptured and had a few months added to his sentence. The Mounties were always glad of a pair of hands to chop firewood.

The Mounties knew little about O'Brien except that he was surly and quarrelsome. When his sentence was up on September 16, he was released. He was penniless, so the Mounties provided him with some food. They had somehow lost a robe he had owned at the time of his arrest, so the police replaced it with one of their own wolf robes.

Free at last from the Mounties and their woodpile, O'Brien hightailed it out of Dawson and headed up the trail along the Yukon River for Selkirk. Somewhere along the way he adopted the alias Tom Miller and hooked up with another Englishman of dubious character — Robert Graves, who was going by the name of Ross. The two settled into camp at Hell's Gates, about eleven miles from Selkirk, claiming to be prospectors. They didn't seem to do much prospecting, but there was a sudden increase in the incidents of thievery, particularly from supply barges that had been caught in the freeze-up of the Yukon River and left unguarded by their owners. Constable Alex Pennycuick of the NWMP post at Selkirk paid "Miller and Ross" a visit on December 11. The two were in possession of a pair of Winchester rifles, a couple of .41 calibre revolvers, and a stock of food. They also had two dogs, one of which was a yellow St. Bernard called Bruce. The pair had a stove that Pennycuick took note of because of the unique design of the draft holes. There wasn't another stove like it in the territory.

"Miller and Ross" were sullen in the presence of the constable, and Pennycuick suspected that everything in their camp, including the dogs, was stolen. But he had no proof. He had to go back to Selkirk to obtain a warrant, and when he returned to Hell's Gates three days later, the two suspects were gone. Pennycuick, a veteran of the British army in India, wasn't too worried. People moving up and down the trails in the Yukon had to turn up in one community or another, and that big yellow dog would be hard to miss. The Mountie could hardly know that the small-time thieves were about to commit a massacre.

On the last Christmas Eve of the nineteenth century, three doomed men were among the guests spending the night at Captain Fussell's Roadhouse at Minto. Lawrence Olsen was a lineman whose job was to patrol and repair the hastily strung telegraph line that was the Yukon's only link to the Outside. Fred Clayson was an American businessman who was a partner with his brother in a mercantile operation based in Skagway. Lynne Relfe, also American, had been working for a Dawson City dance hall called the Pavilion. Clayson and Relfe were on their way to Skagway and were carrying considerable sums of money in cash and gold dust. Relfe also had a peculiar-looking gold nugget that he showed to the other guests at the roadhouse. Olsen was going only as far as Hootchikoo, just a few miles up the trail, to share a Christmas dinner with Constable Patrick Ryan of the NWMP. The three men set off together on the morning of December 25. Except for the men who lay in ambush along the trail, no one ever saw them alive again.

Constable Ryan was concerned when Olsen didn't show up on Christmas Day. It wasn't like the man not to keep an engagement, especially when Ryan was serving up a rare treat in the Yukon — roast turkey. The Mountie knew that in the dead of the Yukon winter even a slight accident in the bush or on the frozen river could be potentially fatal. Over the next couple of days people who had left Minto well after Olsen came into Hootchikoo. Ryan questioned them. Yes, Olsen had left Minto Christmas morning with two other men. No, there was no sign of them on the trail. Some suggested that Olsen might have taken off for a new gold strike at a place called Big Salmon. Ryan didn't think so. Olsen was a responsible man, not the sort to go running off every time some fool yelled "Gold!" And what about the other two — Clayson and Relfe? Clayson was a businessman going to Skagway. Relfe was on his way to join his family back in the United States. *They* wouldn't have gone chasing after pots of gold. Ryan's concern deepened. He could imagine an accident befalling *one* man on the trail, but not *three*! He finally decided to go and look for Olsen himself.

On New Year's Eve, Ryan and a driver set out with a sled and a team of dogs. The constable had a terrible feeling that he was going to have to bring a frozen corpse back to the police post. If necessary, he would search every inch of the trail and the adjoining bush between Hootchikoo and Minto. There was a particularly rough section known as Pork Trail where Olsen could have encountered difficulties if he had plunged into the bush to inspect the telegraph line — if, of course, he had parted company with Clayson and Relfe.

A foot of fresh snow had fallen since Christmas, and to a *cheechako* — a newcomer to the Yukon — any tracks previously made in the snow would have been obliterated. But to an experienced eye, subtle depressions on the surface where new snow had fallen into the footprints in the old snow underneath would still be visible.

For a few hours Ryan searched in the bitterly cold gloom of a Yukon winter morning. Towards noon, about halfway along Pork Trail, he called a halt. While the dogs rested and the driver made a fire for some hot tea, the constable did a little more scouting. Then he found it! Faint evidence of a trail branching south off the main trail into the woods. But it didn't make sense! There was nothing in there but bush — no reason whatsoever for a traveller to leave the trail and head into the trees. In the deadly Arctic winter no sane person just wandered off what amounted to the main highway to take a stroll in the woods. But someone obviously had.

Constable Ryan followed the almost invisible depressions in the snow for a few minutes until he came upon yet another surprise: a tiny, snow-shrouded structure that was a combination of crude log cabin and tent. Ryan thought he had known every habitation between Minto and Hootchikoo, but he had never heard of *this* place. Who could have built it, and why? There was no smoke coming from the chimney pipe. There were no recent footprints in the snow around it, and snow was drifted against the door — sure signs there was no one inside. At least no one *alive*!

Ryan approached the little shelter cautiously. The Mountie had his service revolver, but it was well buried under his parka. He cleared the snow away from the door and pulled it open.

There was no one inside. No injured Olsen, no dead body. In the poor light Ryan did see an empty bunk, a stove, some dishes, a rifle, boxes of ammunition, and piles of canned food in boxes and sacks. The boxes bore the mark of the trading company that owned one of the barges frozen nearby in the river. These were clearly stolen goods.

Ryan knew that Constable Pennycuick had been having trouble with thieves at Selkirk. There could well be a connection here. He would have to wire that officer to come down and take a look. But Ryan still hadn't found any clue concerning the disappearance of Olsen.

It was a mystery why anyone would abandon all that food, a good stove, and a perfectly good rifle. After completing his fruitless search along the trail for Olsen, Ryan arranged to have the shelter watched in case whoever had been using it returned. Then he sent a telegram to Pennycuick.

Alex Pennycuick left Selkirk on the first day of the twentieth century and was in Hootchikoo on January 3. Along the way he had stopped to examine the tent-cabin Ryan had found. He knew right away who had built it. The stove was the same one he had seen in the camp of "Miller and Ross" at Hell's Gates. The scattered plates and eating utensils told him that two men had been staying there. Pennycuick showed Ryan something else he had found in the shelter — a pair of pliers. Ryan recognized the tool as Olsen's.

With a nagging feeling that they might have something more serious than thievery on their hands, Pennycuick sent out descriptions of "Miller and Ross" over the telegraph with instructions that they be apprehended and detained as thieves. There still wasn't much to connect them with the missing men. Then Pennycuick returned to his post at Selkirk. When he got there, he had a message from the NWMP in Dawson. They had received a telegram from Fred Clayson's brother in Skagway. Clayson hadn't arrived there.

One of the Mounties who read the telegraphed descriptions of "Miller and Ross" was Staff Sergeant George Graham in the post at Tagish. It wasn't much of a description to go on: two men of medium height, average build, unshaven. Three-quarters of the sourdoughs in the Yukon looked like that! As it turned out, it wasn't the appearance of one of the suspects that gave the Mounties their first break, but his suspicious behavior.

On January 7, Sergeant Graham was astounded to see a man drive his sleigh and team of horses across the Yukon River at a dangerous spot. From all appearances the man had left the well-travelled main trail in order to avoid passing the police post. Sure enough, the rig struck a thin spot in the ice and one of the horses crashed through. With the help of some other men, the cursing driver got the horse back onto solid ice and then withdrew to the main trail. Graham confronted the man and asked his name.

"George O'Brien," the man answered.

The Mountie examined the sleigh. He saw what appeared to be a bloodstain and a NWMP wolf robe. There was nothing unusual about the bloodstain in a place where men hunted for meat, but the Mounted Police didn't, as a rule, hand out its force-issued wolf robes to civilians. Graham asked O'Brien where he had gotten it.

While his big yellow St. Bernard sat looking on, O'Brien explained that some months earlier he had been in the Dawson jail working on the woodpile. The police there had lost his robe, so they had given him one of theirs. Sergeant Graham coolly told O'Brien he was going to check on that story and instructed him not to leave town. The police would catch up to him if he did. Then he went to telegraph Dawson City.

In addition to the information about the wolf robe, Graham sent full descriptions of George O'Brien, his sleigh and team, and his big yellow dog. The Dawson police wired back that, yes, they had given George O'Brien a wolf robe. Graham was satisfied for the moment that O'Brien's story checked out.

But back in Dawson questions were raised. George O'Brien had left Dawson without a penny to his name. How had he obtained a team of horses? And what about the dispatch they had had from Constable Pennycuick in Selkirk, the one about a suspect named Miller and a big yellow dog? Men in the Yukon often used false names, especially if they were up to no good. It was quite likely that Miller and O'Brien were the same man. The Dawson police wired Taglish again and told Graham to arrest O'Brien as a suspected thief and hold him. Graham's detachment of constables found O'Brien at the home of a Native woman named Jennie, and arrested him.

O'Brien had a bill of sale for the horses, but he couldn't satisfactorily account for how he had come by the money. He had on him a mixed collection of Canadian and American notes, including two $100 bills hidden in his socks. In his sleigh were a Winchester rifle, two Colt revolvers, and a telescope.

By now it was common knowledge in Dawson City and other Yukon communities that three men were missing. Dawson's *Daily News* speculated on the possibility of foul play and openly asked what the Mounties were doing about it. So far the police had no evidence at all that there had been a murder, and only the slimmest circumstantial evidence connecting George O'Brien with the mystery — his stove and Olsen's pliers found in the same rude little shelter, way off the beaten track. But with O'Brien locked up on another charge of theft for the moment, the NWMP began to look for more evidence.

There is an old myth that an outlaw who commits a crime in the wilderness will usually get away with it because the deed will be lost

in the vastness and the isolation. Actually, in a frontier region, especially a frozen one like the Yukon with its relatively small population concentrated in a few communities, the comings and goings of
people are noticed. Strangers always stand out. Word about anything unusual quickly circulates. Mounties asking questions up and
down the river trails soon found witnesses who had seen O'Brien
and Robert Graves (or Miller and Ross) at various places,
particularly in the vicinity of Pork Trail. They had been seen using
the Arctic Express cabin, a little log structure on the river that had
been built for the crews who kept the trail open in winter. The cabin
wasn't far from an ice-bound supply barge that had been pillaged.
Those witnesses who couldn't exactly describe the two men certainly remembered the big yellow St. Bernard. The police interviewers
noted that prior to Christmas Day, 1899, witnesses had seen two
men and a dog, but after Christmas they had seen only one man —
O'Brien. It appeared that Robert Graves, too, was missing.

One witness reported that sometime after Christmas, O'Brien
had tried to sell him a peculiar-looking gold nugget. The description
was the same as that of the nugget seen in Relfe's possession. The
police didn't find the nugget on O'Brien, so he had probably disposed of it. There still wasn't enough evidence on which to build a
case for the prosecution, especially since there were no bodies. And
if the missing men had been killed and their corpses stuffed through
a hole in the ice of the Yukon River, they might never be found.

But whether or not the river had swept the dead men away
on its long journey to the Bering Sea, there was other evidence
to be uncovered. Constable Pennycuick had a good idea to
determine if the mysterious shelter in the bush south of Pork
Trail was indeed the place to look. He took the St. Bernard to a
spot not far from the tent-cabin, unhooked the dog's leash, and
commanded, "Go home!" The big yellow dog bounded off
straight to the shelter, where he settled down in what was obviously a familiar spot and waited for the policeman to catch up.
Now there was no doubt in Pennycuick's mind that this was
O'Brien and Graves's hideout.

With the help of an American private detective named Philip
Maguire, Pennycuick began a systematic search of the shelter and
the surrounding grounds. In the ashes of O'Brien's own stove the

investigators found scraps of burnt clothing, the metal eyelets from moccasins, and belt buckles. When a pair of sled dogs balked at crossing a part of the trail between the shelter and the main trail, they carefully brushed away a few feet of snow and discovered a large pool of frozen blood.

The Canadian policeman and the American private eye now began a meticulous "excavation" of the entire 120 yards of trail leading to the shelter. For several weeks during March and April 1900, they sifted through hundreds of square yards of snow as painstakingly as archaeologists at a dig. They found two more large pools of blood and several smaller ones. Among the many objects they uncovered were empty cartridge shells, buttons, a pair of keys from Fred Clayson's office in Skagway, a dollar bill, a whiskey bottle, a piece of skull, a tooth that had been knocked out by a bullet, Lawrence Olsen's medicine bottle, a receipt made out to Olsen, his lineman's belt, and an axe with three notches in the blade.

Examination of the logs of the shelter and the stumps of cut trees showed that the axe found in the snow had been used to cut all of them. The axe was later identified as O'Brien's by someone who had fitted it with a new handle.

Pennycuick noticed something else about the cut trees. They hadn't been felled strictly for firewood. Twenty-seven trees and the lower branches of numerous others had been removed to provide a clear view of the trails on both sides of the river. A watcher with a telescope or binoculars could observe the approach of travellers for a long distance and, theoretically, set up an ambush. There had been a telescope among O'Brien's belongings.

When Pennycuick and Maguire found cartridge shells, they used line-of-vision calculations to find bullets imbedded in tree trunks. They found other bullets in the ground beneath bloodstained snow. The two men were eventually able to determine which pool of blood had come from which victim by the objects uncovered nearby.

Pennycuick carefully labelled each item and wrote down exactly where it had been found. He staked the location of each find and drew a chart that showed where each object had been uncovered. It was difficult work, crouching almost motionless in the snow and frigid air for long periods of time, often with bare hands exposed to the numbing cold.

As Pennycuick and Maguire sifted through the snow and recorded their findings, the silent trail began to tell its horrific story. O'Brien and Graves had established this place as a bandit lair from which to prey upon travellers. On Christmas morning they had seen Fred Clayson, Lawrence Olsen, and Lynne Relfe hiking from Minto to Hootchikoo. The bandits no doubt knew who Clayson and Relfe were and that they were carrying money. Olsen had nothing of particular value to the outlaws. He just had the bad luck to be in the wrong place at the wrong time.

When the unsuspecting trio reached the bandits' trail, O'Brien and Graves either forced them off the main trail at gunpoint or used some ruse to lure them into the trap — perhaps the promise of a hot cup of tea or a shot of Christmas cheer. As soon as the victims headed up that deadly trail, the killers opened fire.

Clayson was the first to die, perhaps not even knowing what had hit him. A little farther up the trail Relfe went down in a hail of rifle bullets. Evidence in the snow showed that Olsen was pursued up the trail and had put up a struggle. He had been hacked or clubbed and then dispatched with shots from a .41 calibre revolver.

The killers stripped the bodies of anything valuable and tossed aside items that didn't interest them. Snow would soon cover up their bloody work, and who would ever find something like a key in that vast expanse of white? They burned some articles of clothing in their stove and more in an outdoor bonfire.

The murderers hauled the bodies to the river on O'Brien's sleigh for disposal. A piece of thread from a shirt or sweater caught on a twig showed Pennycuick and Maguire where the corpses had been rolled down the bank. The dead men were then shoved through a hole in the ice. It is possible that at this point, with the grim work all done, O'Brien had pulled the ultimate double cross on his partner, because Robert Graves was never seen again.

While Pennycuick and Maguire inched their way along the trail, soldiers of the Yukon Field Force cut and blasted ice from the river so they could drag for bodies. There was a sandbar a short distance from the place where the investigators believed the dead men had been submerged, and they hoped that at least one of them might have been caught on a snag there. This search, however, turned up nothing.

Under the direction of RCMP Superintendent William Scarth in Dawson, the police worked hard to build up the body of evidence against O'Brien. Potential witnesses who had left the Yukon for the Outside were traced and contacted. One was an unsavoury character known, among other names, as George "Kid" West. Kid West was in jail in Seattle and told the police there that he knew something about the murders in the Yukon. He had been in Dawson the previous summer and had done time on the Mounties' woodpile with O'Brien. West said O'Brien had proposed they become partners in a bandit operation along the Yukon trails. They could "clean up a bunch o'coin," as West put it, and "chuck their bodies in the drink." Kid West said he had turned down the offer because he had feared that such misdeeds would bring the wrath of the Mounties down upon a common criminal like himself. Then the police learned that O'Brien had made the same proposition to a labourer named Chris Williams. Williams, too, had refused to be part of such a scheme, but he apparently never thought to tell the police about it.

The Mounties now had plenty of evidence that murder had been planned and brutally carried out, but they still had no bodies. And they could only hold George O'Brien for so long on the theft charge. Then, as the brief northern summer descended upon the gold-rush country, the ice in the Yukon began to break up and the great river gave up its dead.

On May 30 a body was found on a sandbar a mile and a half from Selkirk. It was riddled with bullets and somewhat decomposed, but through clothing and items in the pockets it was identified as that of Fred Clayson. On June 11 another corpse was retrieved from the river eleven miles from Selkirk. It, too, was full of bullet holes. One slug had shattered the jaw and taken out a tooth. The tooth Pennycuick and Maguire had found in the snow perfectly fitted the stump remaining in the mouth. Now the police had hard evidence connecting a body with the trail. Calling cards in a pocket identified the remains as those of Lynne Relfe.

A third body was found near Minto on June 26. The head was little more than a skull, but the prominent teeth enabled people who had known Lawrence Olsen to identify the body as his. Broken ribs and marks on the skull showed that before he was shot, Olsen had been savagely beaten with a blunt object, possibly a rifle butt.

It took time for the police to round up all the witnesses and transport them to Dawson City, so O'Brien's trial didn't begin until June 10, 1901. He was tried only for the murder of Relfe, since that was the only body that could be tied to the crime scene beyond any shadow of a doubt. The prosecution had over 150 pieces of evidence, including sections of logs from the site bearing the distinctive bite marks of O'Brien's axe. Even Bruce the St. Bernard was brought into the courtroom to be identified as the dog that witnesses had seen with O'Brien.

When prosecutor Fred Wade told the court that the Crown would produce witnesses to whom the prisoner had proposed a plan to commit robbery and murder, O'Brien leaped from his chair and cried, "No! They are both policemen and false witnesses!" The "policeman" Kid West had actually been brought from Seattle in handcuffs, complaining all the way.

O'Brien's defence counsel, Henry Bleeker, argued that all of the Crown's evidence was circumstantial, as indeed it was. But the jury members decided that circumstantial or not, the evidence was overwhelming. They deliberated for less than two hours while people waited in the jammed courtroom and dozens more crowded around the outside of the log building. When the jury returned, its verdict was guilty. Justice Dugas sentenced O'Brien to be hanged.

Yukon murderer George O'Brien after his arrest.
(Library and Archives Canada C11526)

Henry Bleeker tried, and failed, to move for a mistrial. When all avenues to save O'Brien's life had been tried, the lawyer told the press quite candidly that in his opinion George O'Brien was "a degenerate, but half man and half savage ... The instincts of a beast of prey and its thirst for blood were born in him." Not exactly the words a condemned man hoping for a last-minute reprieve wanted to hear from his attorney.

In the weeks leading up to the execution date, O'Brien behaved badly in jail. He ranted and raved and defiantly refused to confess to the murders. He made one attempt at suicide but was stopped before he could cheat the hangman.

At 7:30 a.m., Friday, August 23, 1901, George O'Brien went to the gallows, cursing the Mounted Police. He denied his guilt to the very end. Across the country the press applauded the fine work of the NWMP. Toronto's *Globe* boasted that "even the wilderness, with its interminable leagues of loneliness, cannot hide the evil deed and the evil doer from the keen scrutiny of British law."

Before the summer of 1901 was over, another bullet-riddled body was found on a sandbar of the Yukon River. It was far too decomposed for identification, but police strongly suspected it was the corpse of Robert Graves alias Ross. If it was, then both killers had paid the ultimate price for the ambush on a Yukon trail.

10

The Rutledge Gang

A Leap into Eternity

Frank Rutledge first ran afoul of the law one night in December 1888 when he broke into a general store in his hometown of Streetsville, Ontario, and made off with a load of goods. Young Frank, who had been employed at a woollen mill with his brother, was new at this game of burglary and didn't know how to cover his tracks. He simply hightailed it to Toronto with the loot. A county constable became suspicious over Rutledge's disappearance right after the robbery and sent his description to the Toronto police. Rutledge was arrested, sent to Brampton to stand trial at the next assize, and sentenced to four years in Kingston Penitentiary. While awaiting transportation to Kingston, Rutledge slugged a jail guard with an iron bar in a failed escape attempt. That violent little display added another seven years to his sentence. In the summer of 1889 Frank Rutledge entered the brutal prison world at the age of nineteen. When he was released on a pardon only four years later, Rutledge was a tougher and, he thought, smarter criminal. He was also the leader of a gang.

In prison Rutledge had formed a partnership with three other cons: Pat Sherrin, William Black, and Lewis Laurence. These men were doing time for a variety of crimes, including burglary and highway robbery. The gang went on a rampage across Southern Ontario and even paid a short visit to Montreal. In a period of about eighteen months they were believed to have pulled over sixty burglaries.

Their favourite targets were banks, customs houses, and post offices (stolen stamps could be fenced on the black market). Bad luck befell the gang one night when Sherrin was shot dead while they were pulling a job. Before fleeing the scene Rutledge and Black draped a coat over their fallen comrade's body. A touching gesture perhaps, but a mistake. The police identified the coat as Black's and now had a good idea who was responsible for the province's sudden rash of burglaries. Big-city coppers and small-town constables were advised to be on the lookout for the Rutledge Gang.

Rutledge recruited another ex-con, Walter Irving, to replace Sherrin. Then he took the boys on what was supposed to be their most ambitious heist to date — a raid on the Hartman and Wilgriss Bank in Clarksburg, County Grey. Unfortunately for the robbers, they were disturbed before they could penetrate the bank's main vault. But they did get away with a nice haul of silver plate and some rare coins. To throw the police off the trail of the stolen silver, the gang melted it down into bars. The ruse didn't work. When Irving tried to sell a silver bar, he was quickly arrested. In short order Laurence and Black were also picked up and packed off to their old quarters in Kingston. The main quarry, Rutledge, evaded a police stakeout around his family's home in Streetsville and fled to the United States.

Frank Rutledge was next heard of in Red Cloud, Colorado, where he was arrested for stealing a bicycle (Old West lawmen took as dim a view of bicycle thieves as they did of horse thieves). The sheriff found some newspaper clippings about Ontario robberies in Rutledge's pocket and became curious. He wrote to the Toronto police and got a reply that told him all about Rutledge's criminal activities. The letter was read aloud at the Canadian's trial and so impressed the judge that he slapped Frank with a six-year term in Colorado State Penitentiary.

Not one to let prison time go to waste, Rutledge made friends with two fellow inmates who would be the core of his new gang. One went by the name of Thomas Jones. (All of these men used a variety of aliases, and in some instances the authorities never learned their real identities.) Jones was a hard case from Chicago with a long criminal record. He had served prison terms for horse theft and robbery and was said to have killed a man. He was now doing a stretch for his part in blowing a safe while running with an "Indian gang" in Pueblo, Colorado.

The other man, and the youngest of the trio, was Fred Lee Rice. Rice came from a relatively well-to-do family in Champaign, Illinois, and had been to college. He was doing three years for forgery and was suspected of involvement in two bank robberies and a stock scam.

The two Americans and the Canadian agreed that when they were all free they would get together in Chicago and live the high life. They earned time off their sentences for good behaviour and were released within a few months of one another. Rice was the last to get out in early 1900.

For a little while the boys enjoyed the Windy City. They dressed well, lived in better-than-average hotels, and always had cash in their pockets. Their girlfriends — none of whom they told their real names — were from respectable, upscale homes where the ex-cons were always welcome. The young ladies and their parents thought the charming young fellows were businessmen.

The Chicago police knew that anybody associating with Thomas Jones had to be up to no good. But the hands of the police were tied. Whenever they thought they had something on the gang, the word came from somewhere higher up to drop it. Evidently, Jones had connections in strategic places, and the boys were pulling in the kind of money it took to buy off the right people. As one Chicago cop later told Toronto's *Globe*, "They had pull."

A number of different crooks worked with the Rutledge Gang in those early months of the twentieth century — perhaps even Frank's old pal William Black, just released from Kingston. But Rutledge, Rice, and Jones were the three inseparable buddies, alumni of Colorado State Penitentiary. As the summer of 1900 approached, Frank suggested the three of them take a working vacation up north in his old stomping grounds in Canada. He drew them a map of Ontario and showed them the places they could hit on their tour. Rice and Jones agreed, and Fate smiled her wicked smile.

At about 2:00 a.m. on May 23, Toronto police constable Jerrold Ward was on patrol in the Parkdale neighbourhood of the city when he saw four men loitering in front of the Standard Bank. Suspicious, he went over and asked them what they were doing. "None of your business!" was the reply. Suddenly, Ward was staring down the muzzle of a pistol. He looked around and saw a second gunman covering him from behind.

The bandits took Ward's service revolver, pushed his "bobby" helmet down over his eyes, and left him in a barn, tied hand and foot with wire. One of them said that if he made a sound they would blow his head off. While one robber stood guard over the constable, the other three went to work. The men who had just told Ward to be quiet proceeded to make enough noise to wake the dead. The officer heard several loud bangs — the sound of metal hitting metal, he thought. Then all was quiet. A few more minutes passed, and then the man who was guarding Ward hurried away.

A couple of hours later another policeman found Ward trussed up in the barn and released him. The police discovered a sledge-hammer and evidence that someone had tried unsuccessfully to break into the bank. No doubt the racket had attracted attention and the thieves had been obliged to run off.

Two nights later the bandits had better luck. Striking again in the small hours of the morning, they broke into the J.L. Ross Bank in Aurora, just north of Toronto, and took an undisclosed amount of money. Then, to make a good night of it, they robbed the Aurora Post Office. They made their getaway in a horse and rig that had been stolen from in front of a Toronto hotel. The animal was found the next day on its back with its four hoofs tied together and in the air, but otherwise unhurt.

The police were on the scent quickly. They had already heard rumours that Frank Rutledge was in Toronto. Eyewitness descriptions of a man seen in the vicinities of both burglaries, as well as that of a man seen in the stolen rig, convinced them he was their suspect. The police searched the home of Frank's brother and sister-in-law and found evidence that several men had been staying there: clothing, liquor bottles, half a box of cartridges, and some of the stamps from the post office robbery. There was also a railway timetable with writing on it that indicated the birds had flown to Chicago. The Toronto police telegraphed the Chicago police. On June 1, Rutledge, Rice, and Jones were arrested. In their swank hotel room the police found guns and hundreds of dollars in Canadian currency, as well as a new-fangled electronic device believed to be a state-of-the-art tool for cracking safes. The Canadian authorities began the process of extradition. But getting the Rutledge Gang out of Chicago wasn't going to be easy. Thomas Jones still had those connections.

A process that should have taken a few weeks was dragged out a full ten months. The Rutledge boys had the best legal counsel money could buy. Every step of the extradition met with delays, even after the warrant was issued by the U.S. State Department. And the boys had other friends. Letters containing death threats, postmarked Chicago, arrived at Toronto's police headquarters. There were two attempts to smuggle guns to the hoodlums in their cells. One was in a loaf of bread, the other in a pot of pork and beans. A letter found by police in Rutledge's coat in his own handwriting offered $2,000 to anyone who could get him out of jail. A mysterious woman whose real name was never discovered kept trying to visit Jones, but was denied. She kept up a regular correspondence with him, using the name "Kate Spellman." The prisoners wanted her given custody of the property the police had seized in their hotel room. Some people thought she was Jones's girlfriend. Others said she was his sister.

Finally, in April 1901, the Rutledge Gang ran out of options. The last rubber stamp was pounded on the extradition papers. Mindful of the death threats, three Toronto police detectives secretly went to Chicago to escort the gang to Ontario. An editor at Toronto's *Globe* said almost gloatingly that he hoped the three men would be staying in Canada "for a period of years."

Even after they reached Toronto the Rutledge Gang continued to use delaying tactics. The gang members claimed that Jones was ill and couldn't appear in court. They said they had to wait for defence funds to arrive from Chicago. After the initial hearings, it was well into May before the actual trials began.

The press gave the case considerable coverage, dubbing Rutledge, Rice, and Jones "the Chicago Gang." People speculated over a mysterious "Veiled Lady" who sat in the courtroom every day, her face hidden by a black veil. She refused to tell anybody her name. Some thought she was Rice's girl. "Kate Spellman" (who was also present and who had given her name at various times as Maggie Kelly, Maggie Black, and Puss O'Brian) had already been tagged for Jones, and Chicago police claimed that Rutledge, under an assumed name, had married a Chicago girl named Myrtle Norrie. For those who fantasized about bandit romance, that left only Rice for the Veiled Lady.

The jury couldn't reach a unanimous decision on the attempted burglary in Parkdale. The trial carried on, with evidence being presented for the Aurora robberies and horse theft. On the afternoon of Tuesday, June 4, court was adjourned for the day to continue on Wednesday. The prisoners seemed to be in a rather cheerful mood, considering that the Crown had been building a strong case against them. They were taken from City Hall to a horse-drawn cab that would convey them back to jail. The three men were handcuffed together, with Jones in the middle, so that only he had both hands manacled. Sitting inside the hack facing the prisoners were Constable William Boyd, who was old enough to be the father of the prisoners, and Constable Walter Stewart. Seated up top with the driver was Constable Lyman Bogart. Stewart was the only policeman wearing a gun. As the hack pulled away, Rice shouted to the driver, "I think you have a slow team there. Try to drive us home a little faster tonight."

The prisoners regaled the officers with stories as the hack rumbled through the Toronto streets. As they rolled down Gerrard Street towards Sumach, a young man in a blue suit, with a package wrapped in newspaper in his hands, stood waiting on the sidewalk. Bogart and the driver took no notice of him. When

Bandits Frank Rutledge and Fred Lee Rice at the time of their trial in 1901. (Toronto *Globe*)

the hack drew near, the youth calmly walked up to it, tossed the package through the open window, and ran off.

Rice and Rutledge seized the package with their free hands and tore off the paper. Inside the paper was a hat, and in the hat were two revolvers. It all happened so fast that the two startled guards barely had a moment to react. Boyd started to move forward, and Rice shot him through the head from point-blank range, killing him on the spot. Stewart reached for his service revolver, but Rutledge shoved a gun in his face. The constable halted, his fingers touching the butt of his weapon. Jones, the only prisoner without a gun, growled at Rutledge, "Give it to him!"

Mere seconds had passed since Rice had blasted Boyd, and now he, too, had a gun pointed at Stewart. The policeman quickly took his hand away from his gun and said, "I give up! Get out of the rig!"

Fortune was smiling on Walter Stewart that day. Rutledge kicked the door open and leaped from the cab, dragging his two companions with him. He turned and fired several shots into the carriage, hitting nobody. The terrified horses lunged in their harness, and the driver fought to get them under control as they pulled the rig across the streetcar tracks and into the path of an approaching electric trolley. Constable Bogart jumped to the ground, not sure what was happening. The motorman in the trolley brought his vehicle to a stop.

The three bandits made a dash for the trolley as Stewart jumped out of the cab and opened fire on them. Rice and Rutledge shot back and missed, but one of Stewart's bullets struck Jones in the right arm, completely shattering the bone. The gang reached the trolley, and Jones cried with pain as Rice and Rutledge jerked around to fire at Stewart and Bogart, who were moving in on them. Again they missed, and another of Stewart's bullets struck Jones in the groin, staggering him.

Rutledge and Rice dragged their wounded comrade onto the trolley and tried to take over the controls. The motorman, showing more nerve than sense, snatched up the key and refused to surrender it, even after they threatened to shoot him. It was quite likely that both hoodlums were out of bullets. A struggle now developed between the motorman and the manacled bandits, with the badly wounded Jones being wrenched this way and that. The quick-thinking conductor at the rear of the car pulled in the post connecting it to the overhead wire, rendering the trolley inoperable.

The motorman was still fighting with the prisoners. One of them said, "Shoot the bastard!"

The motorman cried, "For God's sake, somebody lend me a hand!"

Two male passengers rushed forward and wrestled with the bandits. By now Stewart and Bogart had reached the trolley and they joined in the melee. Stewart wrenched the gun from Rutledge's hand and clubbed him down with it. The police station was only a few doors away, and more officers rushed to the stranded trolley. They pounded the would-be escapers to a bloody heap. Probably not ninety seconds had elapsed since the package was tossed through the cab window. The young man in the blue suit was never found.

While police officers removed the body of Constable Boyd from the blood-spattered cab, others took the prisoners to the hospital to have their wounds tended. Doctors amputated Jones's mangled arm and removed the slug from his body, but within two days he would be dead. The police arrested Kate Spellman and the Veiled Lady as suspected accomplices in the botched escape attempt. The latter was finally identified as Vina Seavey, a Canadian residing in Chicago. Police suspected that a woman might have been wearing the blue suit. However, the authorities couldn't find any hard evidence against either woman and both were eventually released.

The morning after the shootout Rutledge and Rice were in court on schedule. They were bandaged and their clothes were bloodstained. They weren't at all as chipper as they had been the day before. The jury found them guilty on the robbery charges, and the judge sentenced them to twenty-one years in Kingston Penitentiary. But how much time they would spend in prison was now irrelevant. The following day the court began the hearing on charges concerning the murder of Constable William Boyd. Rutledge was stunned to hear that he was to be tried for murder along with Rice, even though Fred had fired the fatal shot. Ordinarily talkative and swaggering, Rutledge now became silent and morose, though Rice still put on a brave face.

Back in jail that afternoon of June 7, Rutledge and Rice were in a line of inmates being led to the dining room, escorted by only one guard. Rutledge suddenly broke away from the line and bounded up a stairway to a second-storey balcony overlooking a rotunda that was the central part of the jail. The escorting guard, instinctively thinking that Rutledge was making a break, called for help. He got the attention of another guard who was on the second floor, but on the other side of the rotunda from Rutledge. When Rutledge reached the top, he climbed onto the rail so that his back was to the wide-open space. The guard on the opposite balcony cried, "Don't, Frank! Don't do that!"

Thirty-one-year-old Frank Rutledge took one look over his shoulder at the guard. He had spent nine of the last twelve years behind bars. Now he had nothing to look forward to but a noose. In a little chamois bag he wore on a string around his neck — something he had managed to conceal from the guards — was a lock of brown hair tied with pink ribbon, and a picture of a woman. Maybe he thought that everyone would wonder who she was. Let them! Without a word Rutledge launched himself out in a backward dive, a leap into eternity! He struck the stone floor headfirst, cracking his skull like a clay pot. Rutledge died less than an hour later without regaining consciousness. He had cheated the hangman.

Fred Rice wept when he saw Rutledge dead and said, "He was a real man, and he would stick to a friend to the last."

At his trial for the murder of Constable Boyd, Rice tried to lay the blame on Rutledge and Jones, saying he had no knowledge of the planned escape. The jury didn't believe him. He tried to plead self-defence, insisting Boyd threatened him with a gun. But Boyd's daughter testified that her father had left his gun at home that day. On July 18, 1902, Fred Lee Rice, age twenty-seven, went to the gallows. His aged and ailing mother had come from Illinois to be near her son that awful day and to take his body home. She sent him a small bouquet of red and white geraniums the night before the execution. Rice was wearing it in the button hole of his jacket when he took the fatal drop.

One man dead from police bullets, a second by suicide, and a third hanged. Fate had dealt a cold hand indeed to the Rutledge Gang.

TRAIN ROBBER HANEY ROAMING THE HILLS.

Desperado With Price on His Head, Trailed Far by Canadian Officers, Located at Calabasas—Guns Handy Wherever He Goes.

Bill Haney, Train Robber and Gun-fighter,
who has been trailed to the Calabasas hills, where the officers are planning
a campaign to close in and kill or capture him.

Outlaw Bill Haney on the run in a romanticized illustration from the February 20, 1910, edition of the *Los Angeles Times*. Haney was wanted in British Columbia for train robbery and murder. (California State Archives)

11

THE HANEY BROTHERS
Train Robbers

*M*uch has been made of Bill Miner, the notorious American desperado who held up the Canadian Pacific Railway twice in the early 1900s. Canadians have more or less adopted Old Bill as one of their own, as though desirous of having a genuine legendary bandit in the national family. But Miner was neither the first nor the last outlaw to hold up a train in Canada. In 1909 two brothers who weren't convinced that the days of the Old West were over shocked the nation with a daring assault on a CPR train near Ducks, British Columbia. Their names were Bill and Dave Haney. At the time they pulled the job that brought them international notoriety most of the other gentlemen of the train-robbing fraternity were either going grey behind prison walls or pushing up daisies on Boot Hill.

William "Bill" Haney was born about 1871, and Dave around 1873. They grew up in Los Angeles, California, but might have moved there from Kansas or Missouri. Years later a man who married a Haney sister, and regretted it, described the Haneys as "a bad family." The young Haney brothers became well-known to local police, being hauled in on numerous occasions for disturbing the peace, burglary, robbing a milk wagon, and stealing chickens. Dave had his own method for chicken rustling. Using a gas bag and a length of hose, he would anaesthetize the birds so they wouldn't make any noise.

For a time the pair managed to avoid doing any serious jail time, but in April 1894 Bill was sentenced to three years in Folsom

Prison for cleaning out an entire poultry yard. Five years later, in April 1899, Dave was sentenced to five years in Folsom for stealing horses. He was released early for good behaviour in November 1902. A few months later, in January 1903, Bill was in jail in Martinez, California, for some unrecorded felony. He and four other prisoners got hold of a saw and made a successful escape.

For the next few years the record on the Haneys is quiet, but it is almost certain they weren't living the lives of model citizens. There is evidence that they, or at least Bill, roamed around the American West using aliases. If they did spend some time as wandering brigands, they always returned to the Los Angeles area and seemed to have established a stronghold in the nearby Calabasas Hills, where they had a lot of kinfolk. What's more, by the time of the Haneys' raid into Canada, Bill had gained a reputation as a gunfighter. The *Los Angeles Times* reported that he had notches on his gun for men he had killed, though the article didn't say whom or where. The *Times* even compared Haney to the infamous Harry Tracy, one of the toughest, deadliest outlaws in the sagas of the Wild West. Newspapers of the time said that Bill had a bullet scar on one hip and another scar on the back of his head, so he evidently did get into some scrapes.

No one knows just when the Haneys crossed the border into Canada. It might have been days before the holdup; it might have been weeks. A few minutes before midnight on Monday, June 21, 1909, two masked men scrambled across the coal tender of Canadian Pacific's Express Number 97, just east of Ducks, British Columbia. The bandits had probably sneaked aboard at the last water stop. They leaped down into the cab of the locomotive and levelled pistols at the engineer and fireman. One of them told the engineer to stop the train when he saw a signal fire just up ahead.

The engineer did as he was told, and the long passenger train screeched to a halt along the shore of Shuswap Lake. Waiting in the glow of a fire beside the railway were three or four more masked men — witnesses couldn't agree on how many — armed with rifles and pistols. The bandits in the cab ordered the engineer and the fireman out, and one of them fired several shots in the air, apparently to discourage nosy passengers from poking their heads out the windows. Then he gave the fireman the axe from the cab and told him to chop a hole in the door of the first express car.

Otherwise they would blow it open with dynamite. The fireman hacked open a hole big enough for one of the bandits to stick his head inside. After taking a look and exchanging a few harsh words with the astonished express messenger in the car, the bandit made the fireman repeat the procedure with the second express car and the mail car. He didn't see whatever it was he was looking for and told one of his companions, "We got the wrong train."

The leader decided they didn't have time to go through the mail or rob the passengers in the coaches. He told the engineer that everything was all right, then the outlaws piled into a waiting row-boat and pulled off into the darkness of Shuswap Lake.

The engineer and fireman got up a head of steam and took the train into Kamloops to report the bungled holdup. There had, in fact, been a shipment of silver bullion on a train that night, as well as a small quantity of gold. But that cargo had been on train Number 5, which had gone down the line twenty-five minutes ahead of Number 97. The outlaws had indeed missed their train!

Even if the bandits had stopped the right train, railway officials said, they wouldn't have been able to carry off the silver. It had been mixed with lead and was so heavy, according to one railway spokesman, that the bandits would have needed a hundred pack mules to transport it.

The attempted robbery had taken place at almost the exact spot where, just three years earlier, Bill Miner had pulled his second CPR holdup. Memories of the depredations of Old Bill were too fresh in the minds of the railway bosses and the police for them to allow even amateur train robbers to get away with such an outrage. Some police officials actually thought Miner had come back to torment them. Before sunrise the hunt was on.

Native trackers guided posses of British Columbia Provincial Police and civilian volunteers. Some of them were the same men who had helped hunt down Miner and his gang. One was Isaac Decker, a retired provincial policeman who was asked to help out as a special constable. Twenty years earlier Decker had single-handedly captured Texas badman Frank Spencer who was on the run from American law but had made the mistake of killing a man in Canada. Spencer had paid for that on the gallows in the Kamloops jail. Now Decker was glad to help the younger men search for the train robbers. The reward being offered by the CPR may well have been an incentive, too.

As the posses swept through the woods, patrolled the roads, and watched the river crossings, people speculated excitedly on who the desperadoes might be. Some people in Kamloops thought the descriptions given by the train crew of two of the robbers matched those of a pair of strangers who had been hanging around town a week earlier. American police, who were immediately contacted in case the outlaws made for the border, said that the gang might have been the same one that had robbed a Great Northern Railroad train near Spokane, Washington, on May 15. Canadian police suspected that at least two of the CPR holdup men were American.

Although the leaders of the gang *were* American, it is quite likely they had local help, because catching them wasn't the easy task the newspapers initially said it would be. The Native trackers could tell that the robber gang had split up. It was obvious to them, too, that the fugitives weren't just making a blind dash for safety. *Somebody* knew the country pretty well. And they were stealing horses and boats to keep themselves out of the clutches of the law. The fugitives were also getting food from people who either didn't know they were out-laws on the run or were deliberately helping them.

Police officers questioned local farmers and cowboys, making them account for their whereabouts on the night of the holdup. They rounded up hobos, detaining as many as sixty of them for questioning, then brought in bloodhounds and asked the Royal North-West Mounted Police for help. In Calgary and Regina, Mounties boarded trains bound for Kamloops. American detectives arrived, lured by $4,000 in rewards offered by the CPR and the provincial government. However, four days after the holdup the outlaws were still at large.

On the evening of Monday, June 28, Special Constable Isaac Decker at Ashcroft received a tip that three of the fugitives were heading down the Thompson River in a rowboat. He grabbed his rifle and hurried to the river to intercept them. Residents of the vil-lage witnessed what happened, but were unarmed and not able to take any action.

Decker saw a skiff with just two men in it coming down the river. He raised his rifle and shouted at them to come ashore. The men pulled up to the riverbank and climbed out of the boat. One of them had a coat draped over his arm. Only a few feet separated the constable and the suspects. The man with the coat said, "Oh, you would arrest us, eh?"

Suddenly, Decker saw the barrel of a pistol pointing at him from under the coat. He fired, but at the same instant so did the outlaw. Decker's rifle bullet struck the bandit square on the chin and tore through the lower part of his head, killing him on the spot. The slug from the outlaw's gun hit Decker in the thigh. Then the other bandit had a sawed-off shotgun in his hands. He let go with a blast that blew off the top of the constable's skull.

The surviving bandit took some papers from the pockets of his slain companion — to prevent identification — and disappeared into the trees. It was later learned that he avoided capture by the police who descended upon Ashcroft by hiding in an old mining tunnel.

The police had no idea who the dead outlaw was. Even the laundry marks, commonly used by investigators in those days to trace people, had been removed from the clothing. The only clue on the body was a hat with the label of a clothing store in Spokane.

In the fugitive's rowboat the police found a valise in which there were a few sticks of dynamite, a photograph of a little girl sitting on a chair, and a clothes brush with the imprint of the Mercantile Company of Long Beach, California. The police took a photograph of the dead outlaw stretched out on a wooden plank in a shed in Ashcroft and had the picture circulated among police departments in Canada and the United States. The engineer and the fireman from train Number 97 identified him as one of the bandits who had boarded the train and forced them to stop it.

The search intensified for the other man from the rowboat and any other accomplices. Newspapers reported daily that arrests were expected any hour, that it would be impossible for the murderer to escape. But the nameless gunman and his outlaw partners somehow slipped through the army of Native trackers, provincial police, RNWMP, railway police, detectives, and reward-hungry cowboys.

In the first week of July a Spokane deputy sheriff identified the dead train robber in the photograph as Lou Kelly, allegedly a Canadian ex-policeman gone bad. But a strange series of events would prove the deputy wrong.

Canadian police sent the clothes brush and the photograph of the little girl on the chair to the Chicago Police Department. The Chicago police dispatched a detective named Smith to Long Beach with the articles, hoping that someone in the Mercantile Company might be able to tell him something about the clothes brush. No one in that company was any help to him, but when Smith showed the picture around in the Long Beach Police Department, it jogged one man's memory.

A Sergeant Phillips thought there was something familiar about the photo. It wasn't the little girl he remembered, but the chair on which she was seated. He searched his own files and found a duplicate of the picture. It had been used two years earlier in a search for the child, who had been a runaway. The police located the photographer in Los Angeles, and from him learned the name of the woman who had brought the child in to have her picture taken. The woman told the police she had given the picture to a man named Haney. Thus, the investigators found themselves in the home of the Haney

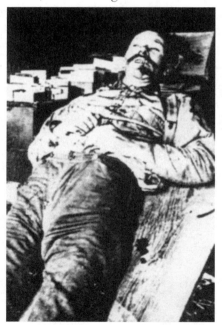

Bandit Dave Haney lies dead after a shootout with British Columbia constable Isaac Decker. Constable Decker was also killed. (Vancouver *Daily Province*)

brothers' father. There on the mantelpiece was a photograph of the same man who had been killed by Constable Decker in Canada. The dead man was Dave Haney. His companion in the rowboat, the man who had blown Decker to kingdom come with a shotgun, had been his big brother, Bill.

It was August by the time all this sleuthing had been done. Canadian detectives went to Los Angeles to collaborate with their American counterparts, but they could find no trace of Bill Haney. There were newspaper reports that the Canadians pursued the California bandit all over the American West and into Mexico, but this may just have been yarn spinning on the part of the writers. Not until February 1910 did the Los Angeles police receive a tip on Haney's whereabouts.

An informant, no doubt with an eye on the $4,000 price on Haney's head, told the police that the wanted man was in the Calabasas Hills, hiding out with relatives. The Americans and the Canadians devised a plan to trap Haney at the home of his half-sister up in the hills, but Haney was warned of the scheme, probably by his half-sister, and evaded capture.

It was no secret now that the outlaw was in the hills above Los Angeles, playing a heady game of hide-and-seek with the law. The *Los Angeles Times* ran a somewhat embroidered feature, complete with a dime-novel-type illustration depicting Haney as a romantic desperado, telling the story of the now internationally famous outlaw: "A lone horseman, with six-shooter in easy reach and his rifle slung over his saddle horn, rides silently about Calabasas. His well-knit body sits well on the bronco. His round, weather-beaten face looks placid enough, but his blue eyes constantly pierce each tree or clump of bushes where a person might hide. He is 'Bill' Haney."

The article gives a fanciful account of the train robbery, including a running gunfight between the outlaws and the Mounted Police, in which *two* policemen are killed. It goes on to relate how Haney rules the hill country like a bandit king: "Never did an outlaw terrorize a community more thoroughly.... He is the monarch of the hilly district and everywhere a royal homage is paid to him. He reigns not because he is loved, but [because] there are notches on his six-shooter and he has well earned the title of 'gun man.'"

If Haney read the account, he might well have developed a swelled head. It was the sort of thing people had once written about such celebrated outlaws as Jesse James and Billy the Kid. Haney might also have thanked the *Times* for letting him know — if he wasn't already aware — that the Calabasas Hills were swarming with men looking for him. There were not only the "most skilled secret service men" of the Canadian government, according to the *Times*, disguised as "meek-looking strangers ... dressed as Englishmen" on his trail, but also sheriffs and deputies who had taken leaves from their regular duties to go after the outlaw. The hills were, in fact, alive with would-be bounty hunters, especially after the CPR raised the reward to $5,500! California editors predicted, as their Canadian colleagues had done eight months earlier, that Haney would be taken within a matter of days, though not without a fight.

But the quarry still proved to be slippery. The sheriffs, deputies, private detectives, and bounty hunters searched the hills for weeks on end and returned to Los Angeles dirty, footsore, and empty-handed. One pair of deputies who told the press that they had "almost" captured the outlaw received a taunting letter from Haney: "I was on the trail next to you. You had better stay in the city where you have only city folks to deal with."

Nonetheless, not all of Haney's kinfolk in the Calabasas Hills were on his side. The *Times* reported that a female relative of the outlaw had been in communication with the police and had expressed her willingness to help give him "his just deserts." The newspaper said: "The fugitive does not suspect that she is willing to betray him, and it is likely that he would not hesitate to add her to

$2,500 REWARD

By the Provincial Government for the arrest and conviction of the four men who held up the C. P. R. train seven miles east of Ducks Station about midnight on Monday, the 21st June, 1909.

DESCRIPTION

The leader is a man about 5 ft 7 or 8 inches, weighing 140 to 145 pounds, black cutaway coat and brown overalls, has small feet and hands. The others are larger men, wearing heavy boots.

WENTWORTH F. WOOD, Sheriff.

A poster offering a reward for the apprehension and conviction of the Haney brothers and their gang. (British Columbia Archives B-00726)

the victims listed by notches on his gun if he had an intimation that she would give him up."

One can only wonder what the woman felt when she read this in the newspaper. After all, if Bill didn't read it himself, someone would surely tell him about it. But it seemed she wasn't the only one in the hills who wanted to be rid of the bandit. The *Times* went on: "The whole population of the Calabasas Hills is anxious that Haney should be taken away, and several residents have recently overcome their timidity enough to give the officers information as to where Haney was last seen, and what they know of him."

At some point the fugitive must have grown weary of constantly looking over his shoulder and jumping every time a twig snapped, because he quietly slipped out of the Calabasas Hills. In March he was seen in El Centro in the southern part of California, near the Mexican border. When detectives arrived there, they discovered he had been working on a ranch in the Imperial Valley but had fled well ahead of them.

For months nothing was heard of Haney, though lawmen on horseback and in automobiles continued to infest the Calabasas Hills. On August 4 the *Times* reported that Haney was in Los Angeles, with the police hot on his trail. Then on August 10 the paper reported that Bill Haney had been caught not in California, but in Montana!

While the manhunters were doing everything but level the Calabasas Hills trying to find him, Haney had been heading east. On August 9, 1910, he rode into the town of Dillon in the southwestern corner of Montana, mounted on a fine bay horse. He had grown a moustache and a full beard and was wearing a long brown wig under his hat. His overalls gave him the look of a farmer or prospector. He started a fire in a barn, then shouted the alarm himself. While most of the townsmen ran to fight the blaze, Haney entered the State Bank of Dillon and told the lone clerk, A.J. Breda, that he needed to make change. Breda looked aside to open the cash drawer, and when he glanced up again, he was staring into the muzzle of a .32 Colt automatic. "Throw up your hands," the robber commanded.

Instead, Breda ducked under the counter and scrambled for the back door. "I'll shoot!" the bandit warned. The clerk kept going and made it to the door. Haney shot at him, the bullet harmlessly striking an account book. Breda made it to the outside, slammed the door, and locked it, then ran shouting that the bank was being robbed.

Haney bolted out the front door, not a penny richer than when he had gone in. He jumped onto his horse and spurred it to a gallop. The bandit might well have made his getaway, but when his horse hit a paved section of road at full speed, its hoofs slid. The animal went crashing down, and Haney was thrown to the ground with such force that he was momentarily knocked out. Two private citizens held him down until Deputy J.F. Wikidal came running up to disarm the bandit and take him into custody. Besides the .32 automatic, Haney was carrying a .45 Colt. There would likely have been bloodshed in Dillon if he had had a chance to shoot it out.

Dragged off to the jailhouse of Sheriff Gosman, Haney was placed under arrest for arson (the barn burned down), attempted robbery, and assault with a firearm. A search of the prisoner turned up a hundred rounds of ammunition, a gold watch, two letters written in code (which no one would be able to decipher), and a total of $2.65. There was nothing on the man or on his horse to provide a clue about his identity except "E. Smith" marked on his undershirt. The prisoner eventually gave his name as Edward Smith.

But Haney's spate of bad luck wasn't over. There was a man in Dillon who had known Bill Haney in Los Angeles and recognized him despite the beard. He informed Sheriff Gosman that the prisoner in his jail was Bill Haney and was wanted in California. The man also said Bill Haney was wanted in British Columbia where he and his brother, "Dan," had robbed a train and killed a policeman, with "Dan" himself being shot dead. The following morning the sheriff entered the bandit's cell and said, "Hello, Bill. Where's your brother Dan?"

For a moment the prisoner seemed startled. Then he said, "I haven't any brother Dan."

The sheriff replied, "Well, you used to have."

The telegraph wires linking Los Angeles, British Columbia, and Dillon fairly hummed with activity. The description of the man in Gosman's jail tallied with that of the much-wanted Haney: size and build, facial features, moles on his face and body, bullet scar on one hip. Police in Los Angeles and British Columbia asked if Sheriff Gosman could provide them with a photograph of his man.

In his cell Haney refused to get off his cot, complaining he had been too badly injured in the fall from his horse. He had, in fact, coughed up blood, or so it appeared, but a doctor examined him and said he didn't have any serious injuries. Nonetheless, Haney moaned constantly and made a big show of being in great pain. He had to be forcibly dressed and carried to the town courthouse for a hearing before a judge. When the judge tried to speak, Haney drowned him out with yells and loud groans.

Haney was just as uncooperative when a photographer tried to take his picture. He pushed his chin to his chest, squinted his eyes, and opened his mouth wide. Even when deputies yanked his head back by the hair so that he had to look into the camera, he squirmed so much that the images were spoiled. Most cameras of the time still required a subject to be very still so that a recognizable image could be made.

Sheriff Gosman soon had reason to believe that Haney had confederates who would try to spring him. There were strange lantern signals seen in the vicinity of the jail at night, and pistol shots that couldn't be accounted for. One morning the sheriff found a crowbar hidden in a corner of the corridor near Haney's cell. It had evidently been dropped in through a window. The sheriff decided to take advantage of the modern technology of the time to thwart any jail-break attempts. He hooked up the bars on the jail windows with the building's electric lighting system. Then he put warning notices up inside the jail, but nothing on the outside, hoping that some friend of Haney's would "receive something worse than a mule kick." One night the lights in the jail did flicker because of some apparent tampering at a window. Well-armed deputies turned out to investigate, but whether or not some would-be intruder got a shocking surprise and was dragged away by accomplices, Gosman never knew.

As the weeks went by, the problem of identifying "Ed Smith" took some strange turns. The man who had first fingered the prisoner as Bill Haney had no doubt whatsoever. However, a detective from California who travelled to Dillon said the prisoner *looked* like Bill Haney, and he was certain the bay horse was Haney's, and he *thought* he recognized the outlaw's equipment as Haney's, but he just wasn't sure. A Canadian detective went to Dillon, but he had never seen either Haney brother and couldn't make a positive identification. He said the Canadian police weren't even sure if the dead outlaw in British Columbia was Dave or Bill.

Then something about the situation in Dillon intrigued the chief of police in Dubois, Idaho. He sent Sheriff Gosman a photograph of a man known as Fred Taylor ... and Frank Jones ... and Dr. Dobbs ... and Ed Smith. The man had a reputation as a big spender, and people in Dubois used to wonder where he got his money. He was suspected of being involved in a robbery in Salmon, Idaho, but no one could prove anything. Sheriff Gosman believed the man-of-many-names in the Idaho photograph was the same Ed Smith he had in his jail. He had the photograph circulated to see if it would bring in more information. It did.

The city marshal of Kemmerer, Wyoming, arrived in Dillon after seeing the Idaho photograph in the newspaper. *He* identified the prisoner as Martin Foley, a former member of Butch Cassidy's Wild Bunch, who had served time in prison in Wyoming for manslaughter.

Canadian officials had no doubt that an American outlaw named Bill Haney had held up the CPR and killed Special Constable Decker. But failing to positively identify the man in the Dillon jail as Haney, they didn't have much chance of extraditing him. Montana authorities weren't sure if the man was Ed Smith, Bill Haney, Fred Taylor, Frank Jones, Dr. Dobbs, Martin Foley ... or someone else. What they knew for certain was that a man who called himself Ed Smith had ridden into Dillon where he burned down a barn, tried to rob a bank, and took a shot at an unarmed clerk. They tried him as Ed Smith and sentenced him to twenty years in the state penitentiary in Deer Lodge, Montana. The *Los Angeles Times*, nonetheless, reported that the man they had locked up was Bill Haney.

On February 15, 1920, Bill Haney — for the Dillon bank robber was in all likelihood he — was paroled after serving a little more than nine years of his sentence. At that point he vanished from history. No one was ever brought to trial for the CPR holdup or the murder of Isaac Decker.

12
WILLIAM RUTTAN
Murder in Muskoka

William Ruttan wasn't a proud father of the bride. In fact, the fifty-year-old man, nicknamed "Black Billy" by his neighbours because of his dark hair and swarthy complexion, was furious. Entirely against his wishes, his twenty-one-year-old daughter, Mina, had married Alfred Coutermanche at the end of April 1914. Now they were living with Alfred's older brother, George, and his wife and children in a house at Housley's Rapids in Ryde Township, about twelve miles from Bracebridge, Ontario. The Coutermanche house was only half a mile from Ruttan's farm.

Ruttan's neighbours all said he was "a fair man," though he much preferred hunting in the woods to working his farm, and his family lived on the brink of destitution. But he couldn't accept Mina's marriage to young Coutermanche, and there was apparently more to it than just a daughter's disobedience. Mina had evidently shared a dark secret with her new husband.

For the first three weeks after the wedding, the old man harassed the young couple. Finally, Alfred went to Bracebridge to lay a charge against Mina's father — incest! Unfortunately, there was no one in town who could go out immediately and arrest William Ruttan. The Muskoka region was in the midst of a sensational murder investigation, and all of the local authorities were in nearby Honey Harbour for the inquest. This bit of unlucky timing would have tragic consequences.

Somehow Black Billy heard about what his despised son-in-law was doing in town. The Ruttan family already had trouble with the law. Two sons were at that moment sitting in the Bracebridge jail on a charge of cruelty to an animal. They had beaten a cow to death! Something in Black Billy snapped, and he made up his mind to wipe out the whole Coutermanche family.

At seven o'clock on the morning of May 20, George Coutermanche and his wife, Eva, were outside their small frame house, cleaning some fish George had caught the night before. Their three children were inside, still in bed, as were Mina and Alfred. Ruttan had crept through the bush and was hiding behind a stump a short distance away. He was armed with an "over and under," a gun that was a combination rifle and shotgun. Black Billy had the reputation of being one of the best shots in Muskoka. He calmly stood up, aimed, and fired the rifle.

The bullet missed, and George looked up from his fish-gutting to see where the shot had come from. Ruttan fired again, this time with deadly accuracy. The slug tore through the heart of thirty-two-year-old George Coutermanche, and he fell dead at his wife's feet. Eva screamed at Ruttan not to shoot her husband again, but when she saw him reload, she turned and dashed for the house. Ruttan squeezed off another shot that missed, then ran after her.

With Ruttan right on her heels, Eva flew through the door, slammed it in his face, and locked it. Ruttan crashed into the door, then began to break it in. Eva retreated to a bedroom, where Alfred and Mina had been awakened by the shooting and the screams. Black Billy came crashing through the front door and went straight for the bedroom. He tried to force the door, but the three people on the other side held it closed. Ruttan fired a shot through the door, and the bullet skinned Mina's finger. The enraged man fired again, and this time the bullet struck his daughter in the neck. Mina collapsed, dying, in Alfred's arms.

Eva was hysterical. Terrified that Ruttan would get into the room, she smashed a window and climbed out into the yard. Ruttan probably didn't hear the sound of breaking glass, since he was almost deaf, but he must have guessed his quarry might try to escape through a window, because he rushed out of the house and around to the back. He saw Eva before she could find a hiding place and shot her in the knee. Delirious with pain and fright, Eva crawled behind a woodpile. Black Billy could have finished her off, but the Coutermanche he wanted to kill most of all was still in the house.

Ruttan ran back inside and fired another shot through the bedroom door. Alfred had pressed himself flat on the floor, so the bullet missed. But at any moment the crazed gunman would realize there was nobody holding the door closed. Barefoot and dressed only in whatever he had worn to bed, Alfred crawled out through the window his sister-in-law had smashed and sprinted across the yard for the bush. Ruttan kicked open the bedroom door and saw him. He sent three rifle bullets whistling after the fleeing figure, but the young man made it to the trees unhurt.

The murderous father would also have seen his daughter dead on the floor. Ruttan didn't pursue Coutermanche, and he seemed to have forgotten about Eva, still cringing in agony behind the woodpile. He set fire to the Coutermanches' stable, then sat on a stump to watch it burn. George and Eva's three frightened children watched him from their bedroom window. By the time Alfred came back with help, Black Billy was gone.

Police arrived from Bracebridge and Gravenhurst, and Inspector William Greer, one of the top detectives with the Ontario Provincial Police, was sent to take command of the manhunt. Men were sworn in as special constables, even though they were clearly apprehensive about going into the bush after Ruttan. The man knew the woods, and no one doubted he wouldn't give up without a fight. The latter was confirmed when Greer went to Ruttan's house the day after the shooting and spoke to his wife.

The distraught woman told Greer that her husband had paid her a midnight visit. He told her, with much weeping, that he had killed their daughter. "I did not mean to kill her," he cried. Ruttan swore that if Alfred Coutermanche went to the cemetery for Mina's burial he would shoot him on sight. He said that if he could kill Coutermanche he would gladly accept the consequences. Then he ranted about the police holding his sons for killing a cow. After that he ate a meal and had his wife make him a bundle of sandwiches. Then he kissed her goodbye and said, "You may never see me alive again."

Black Billy apparently believed he had other scores to settle. In the small hours of the morning, after leaving his home, he burned down the barns of two of his neighbours, as well as a third neighbour's warehouse. Three horses and a cow died in one of the barn fires. Fear descended upon the whole Muskoka region. Schools were closed, and farmers resolved to guard their property at night with loaded guns until Ruttan — now called "outlaw" by the press — was captured or killed.

All day Friday, May 22, police officers and armed civilians tramped through the bush but couldn't find the killer. As evening approached, Greer placed several men around Ruttan's house to watch it from places of concealment. He told them that if any of them saw *anybody* approach the house they were to signal the others immediately and then apprehend the person. Greer didn't tell Mrs. Ruttan about the stakeout.

Early in the evening the police saw Mrs. Ruttan leave the house. An hour later she returned. At about 10:30 p.m. two of the watchers saw someone approach the house in the darkness. The figure appeared to be wearing a dress. The officers decided it was a woman, and ignoring Greer's orders, they let the person pass unchallenged. They later concluded that Mrs. Ruttan had stashed a dress in the woods so her husband could disguise himself.

Mrs. Ruttan was cooking pancakes when Black Billy entered the house. He immediately demanded something to eat and told one of his young daughters to keep watch and listen for any noises outside. He said again that he wanted to "riddle his son-in-law with bullets" and added that once that was done he would deprive the police of the pleasure of capturing him alive. He had been in the house only a few minutes and was devouring half-cooked pancakes when the little girl said, "Dad, I hear a noise outside."

Ruttan picked up his gun and crept out the back door. Two policemen stood about twenty-five yards away. One of them raised his revolver and squeezed the trigger, but the gun misfired. The second officer couldn't risk a shot because the other constable was in the way. Ruttan plunged into the night woods. Now the officers let go with a volley of about ten shots, but none of them struck the fugitive. No doubt there was hell to pay when Greer was told how the two sentries had bungled their assignment.

The funeral for Mina and George Coutermanche was held the next day. The service was in a private home, then there was a three-mile ride, part of it through the woods, to Parkway Cemetery. Alfred Coutermanche wanted to go with the bodies of his wife and brother to the graveyard, but Greer wouldn't permit it for fear that Black Billy would be waiting in ambush. He left Coutermanche at the house with two constables, while he himself accompanied the funeral procession, perhaps hoping the outlaw would show himself. Nine constables armed with shotguns were along in case he did. But a heavy, cold rain came down and there was no interruption of the sad ceremony by the killer. A local woman later reported seeing Ruttan skulking in the woods on her property, not far from the cemetery. In all likelihood, with the roofs of the horse-drawn buggies raised against the pouring rain, Ruttan wouldn't have been able to see if his intended victim was among the mourners.

Warm weather often comes late to Muskoka, and that spring of 1914 was a cold and wet one. The men Greer had beating the bushes found the going miserable, and the inspector knew that Ruttan must be having a decidedly unpleasant time hiding and running. Hunger and exposure, he was sure, would force the fugitive out into the open. The day after the funeral Greer was rewarded.

By Sunday morning Black Billy was so weak from cold, hunger, and lack of sleep that he could barely crawl out of the bush to his house. He had discarded his gun because he could no longer carry it. His clothes were soaked and his fingers were frostbitten. He awakened his wife and told her to make him something to eat. Then he sat down to what he said was the most satisfying meal he had ever eaten. He told Mrs. Ruttan that he was ready to surrender to the police. Ruttan didn't have long to wait. They were already at the door.

When Greer walked in, Ruttan bade him a cheerful good morning and told the inspector he needn't be afraid, because he was giving himself up. He added, though, that if the weather hadn't been so nasty he would have held out longer. The idea of clearing out of Muskoka altogether didn't seem to have occurred to Ruttan. He told Greer that the night he had escaped into the woods with the police shooting at him was "the most adventurous experience of my life."

As he wolfed down his food, Black Billy explained how he had kept out of the searchers' way in the woods by avoiding his familiar haunts, which he knew his neighbours would show to the police. He said there were some people he would like to get even with, but he especially regretted not getting another chance to kill his son-in-law. Ruttan gave Greer some rifle cartridges and shotgun shells he had in his pocket, saying he had been saving them for Alfred Coutermanche. The killer didn't say a word about murdering his own daughter but did express a wish to see her grave. He kissed his wife and children goodbye, then left with the police.

At his trial, held in Bracebridge the following October, Black Billy presented more of a pathetic figure than a sinister one. Because of his deafness he could hardly hear a word that was said. He refused counsel, pleaded guilty, then on the advice of the judge changed his plea to not guilty. When Eva Coutermanche was on the stand, he complained about how the woman "kept" Mina at her house. It took the jury only seventeen minutes to find him guilty but with a recommendation for mercy. The judge sentenced Ruttan to hang, but Black Billy didn't go to the gallows. Accepting a petition signed by many Muskoka residents, the Canadian government commuted the death sentence to a prison term. By this time the carnage in Europe that would be called the Great War had started, and the murders in the backwoods of Muskoka would be pushed out of mind by even greater horrors.

13 SIBERIAN OUTLAWS IN CANADA
Gunfight in New Hazelton

In the bullet-riddled, gun-smoke-shrouded history of the American Wild West, there were two occasions in which the ordinary citizens of frontier communities stood up to marauding outlaw gangs. The first took place on September 7, 1876, when the notorious James-Younger Gang rode into Northfield, Minnesota, to rob a bank and limped out empty-handed and bloodied, leaving two of their number dead in the street. The second happened when on October 5, 1892, the Dalton Gang swept into Coffeyville, Kansas, with the intention of robbing two banks at the same time. Only one of them left town, wounded and bound for prison. The other four were dead, shot full of holes by angry townspeople. Both those dramatic incidents have achieved legendary status in Old West lore and have inspired many books and films.

On the Canadian frontier the ordinary citizens were usually content to let the duly authorized officers of the law handle the business of bringing outlaws to bay. But on an April morning in 1914, in the little railway construction town of New Hazelton, British Columbia, an attempted bank robbery exploded into one of the wildest gunfights ever to take place north of the Forty-ninth Parallel. Leading the side of the law was not a steely-eyed sheriff, nor even a stalwart Mountie, but a veterinarian who also preached on Sundays. His adversaries weren't hard-riding desperadoes in black Stetsons, but an unlikely collection of bandits from the other side of the world. The story of their leader's journey to the woods of northern British Columbia could itself be the stuff of an epic tale.

Dzachot Bekuzaroff was from Siberia. There, according to the men who would become his partners in crime in Canada, he was leader of a bandit gang until he was captured and banished to a penal colony on Sakhalin Island, north of Japan. Bekuzaroff got a lucky break in 1905 when Russia lost a war with Japan and had to cede the southern part of the island to the Japanese. The victors freed the Russian prisoners on their half of the island, one of them being Bekuzaroff.

Rather than return to Russia, Bekuzaroff boarded an American ship that was recruiting cheap labour for railway construction in Mexico. Considering his background, it wasn't likely that as the ship made the long voyage across the Pacific Ocean, the bandit chief was looking forward to life as a common labourer.

From Mexico, Bekuzaroff drifted north to San Francisco, and then to Vancouver. He gathered a gang of fellow Russians, some of whom were from Siberia. The group of six or seven men were either picking up work where they could find it or were living by thievery of one sort or another as they headed into the B.C. interior, making plans to rob a bank.

One evening in early November 1913 Ray Fenton, an Englishman recently arrived in the B.C. wilderness, had just finished supper and was returning to work with nineteen-year-old Jock McQueen. Fenton was chief cashier at the Union Bank of Canada in New Hazelton, and McQueen, fresh from Scotland, was his clerk. Fenton unlocked the door of the sturdy log bank building and the two stepped inside. No sooner had they entered than a "funny, foreign voice," as Fenton later described it, told them, "Get your hands up!"

Fenton obeyed instantly, but McQueen, apparently thinking it was some local boys pulling a prank, was slow to comply. One of the robbers shot him in the head, and the young Scot fell bleeding at Fenton's feet.

The bandits made Fenton light a lamp and then ordered him to open the strongbox. When he told them he didn't have the combination, they started shooting into the floor at his feet. "They were trying to scare me," he said later. "They didn't need to. I was plenty scared."

Fenton couldn't see how many were in the gang, but guessed they had entered the bank through an unlocked back window. Finally satisfied the frightened cashier really didn't know the combination, the bandits dragged the strongbox out of the room that served as a vault and hauled it out the back door. One of the bandits pushed Fenton into a tiny back bedroom and told him to get on the bed and stay there for an hour or he would be shot.

Two minutes later Fenton heard McQueen cry, "Ray! Ray!" Not knowing if any gunmen were still in the building, Fenton jumped off the bed and hurried out. The robbers had gone, leaving the back door open. The rush of cold air had revived McQueen, who lay in a pool of blood with a bullet hole in his head above his eye. Fenton grabbed the bank's gun, ran outside, and fired six shots in the air to sound the alarm.

News of the robbery spread quickly through the little wood-and-canvas town. One of the first to arrive at the bank was Donald "Doc" MacLean, who was both veterinarian and preacher. It would take half an hour for a regular doctor to reach the scene, so MacLean did what he could to stop the bleeding from Jock McQueen's head.

Doc MacLean was a man who walked tall in New Hazelton. He was a real gentleman, kind-hearted and liked by everyone. But he was no pantywaist Bible thumper. MacLean, thirty-three, was over six feet tall, lean and muscular, and a crack shot with a rifle. Originally from Nova Scotia, he had spent some time in Alberta tending to sick and injured horses and busting broncs. There he had been instrumental in sending a rustler to jail. When the rustler got out, he warned MacLean he would be gunning for him. Doc's laconic reply would have suited a character out of a Zane Grey novel. "Don't miss, Tom," he said, "because I won't."

There was only one policeman in New Hazelton, and like so many other residents, he was a newcomer. As two doctors from the nearest hospital arrived to take McQueen into their care, some of the men started talking about forming a posse to go after the bandits and "string 'em up!" Cooler heads convinced the potential vigilantes that chasing after armed men in the bush at night would be foolhardy. The next day groups of men fanned out across the countryside looking for signs of the bandits. They found the remains of a camp and the smashed-open strongbox but nothing more. The outlaws got away with $16,000. Not long after, Jock McQueen died.

All anyone knew about the desperadoes was that they were "foreigners." That wasn't much to go on, because in the towns, timber shanties, and mining camps of British Columbia there were men from every nation under the sun. Five months later, however, the people of New Hazelton were certain the same gang paid their town a return visit.

At about 10:30 on the morning of April 7, 1914, Doc MacLean was walking to the town well with a bucket in his hand. New Hazelton had a celebration planned for that day. The Grand Trunk Pacific Railway, the main reason for the town's existence, was completed, and a crowd was at the tiny railway station awaiting a trainload of dignitaries. At the opposite end of town the new steel vault in the bank was stuffed with money for the construction workers' last big payday. E.B. Tatchell, the bank manager, was outside near a corner of the building, talking to a friend. Inside the bank were Ray Fenton and Robert Bishop, a clerk.

Beside the pump MacLean was heading for was a large boulder of silver ore sitting on a squat wooden pedestal. It was a rough monument to British Columbia's mineral wealth. This chunk of ore was about to become a key position in a gun battle that rivalled the storied shootout at the OK Corral in its violence and left just as many bodies in its wake.

Nobody paid any attention to the seven men who walked abreast up the muddy main street of New Hazelton, heading straight for the bank. Not the people at the train station and not Doc MacLean. The seven men were scruffy and all wore long coats, but that could be said of many of the labourers in town. The men could have been there for the celebration or just to pick up their pay. Only later would Doc's wife, Eva, recall that the night before she had encountered the same men on the street. They were all drunk, and one pulled another off the wooden sidewalk to give her room to pass, saying, "Get out of the lady's way, ya big bum!" Mrs. MacLean recalled that it had seemed amusing, because the offender had fallen on his backside in the mud. But she found nothing funny at all about those men the following day.

The seven men probably passed Doc MacLean as he strolled to the well. They certainly would have passed manager Tatchell as they entered the bank. He took no notice of them, nor they of him. Inside the bank, cashier Fenton was talking to Al Gaslin, the town postmaster, when a bad dream he wanted to forget barged in. Five of the men had pistols and the sixth pulled a rifle from under a long coat. A seventh man out on the front step also had a rifle. One of the bandits barked in a thick Russian accent, "This is a holdup! Get your hands in the air!"

The startled men raised their hands. Gaslin was holding some cash and a few cheques, which a bandit snatched from him. The postmaster told the bandit the cheques would be no good to him, but the thief stuffed them into his pocket, anyway. Then the gang began cleaning out the cash drawers.

The image of Jock McQueen's bloody face flashed into Fenton's mind. What if the bandits decided to gun down another defenceless man! The bank's gun was in the small back bedroom, and Fenton was right by the door. He suddenly dived through the door and grabbed the pistol. One of the bandits followed him and then ducked back into the office when he saw the gun in the cashier's hand. At the same moment Fenton squeezed the trigger, and the gun jammed. Quickly, he slammed the door shut and wedged the bed against it.

In the office the bandits told Bishop to open the safe. He said he didn't have the combination — only the manager did. One of the robbers fired several shots into the floor at his feet. Immediately, another bandit cursed and called his colleague a fool. "You'll have the whole town in here," he growled.

Outside, Tatchell was startled by the sound of gunshots from inside the bank. He hurried to the front door and was warned away by the outlaw standing guard with the rifle. The man obviously didn't realize this was the only person in town who could open the safe. Tatchell darted around the corner of the building and ran for help. Later he said he headed straight for Doc MacLean because the veterinarian knew how to handle a gun. The town's lone policeman wasn't even in New Hazelton that morning.

Tatchell spotted MacLean just as Doc reached the town pump. "Another holdup, Doc!" the manager cried, intercepting him. "Get your gun!"

With Tatchell right behind him, MacLean dropped the bucket and dashed for the tent he and Eva were using as a temporary home. He grabbed a .44 Colt revolver and tossed it to Tatchell, then stuffed a handful of cartridges into his pocket and picked up his rifle, a British army Lee-Enfield .303. Doc told Eva to stay inside, then he and Tatchell hurried out to the street. Eva didn't stay inside, though. She went out to see what was going on. Years later she would write about the day's events in her book *The Far Land*.

Word that the bank was being robbed again swiftly spread through a town that was still angry over the murder of young Jock McQueen. MacLean and Tatchell took cover behind the big silver ore boulder as the Russian in front of the bank began shooting down the street. Other townsmen armed with pistols, rifles, and shotguns scrambled to firing positions. One of them, fittingly, was known as "Arizona" Smith.

In the bank there was confusion as the robbers realized the town had been alerted. Some of the bandits wanted to make a break for the bush. Others wanted to make a stand inside the protection of the bank. Fortunately for Bishop and Gaslin, the idea of taking hostages apparently didn't occur to the robbers. Then the man outside cried for help because he was being outgunned. The gang made its decision and piled out the front door, guns blazing.

The lookout man tried to draw a bead on Doc, but his bullet ricocheted off the silver ore. Doc fired back and killed the lookout with one bullet. Another of the bandits tried to retrieve the lookout's rifle, and Doc put a bullet through his leg, crippling him.

By now the main street of New Hazelton looked and sounded like Dodge City thirty years earlier. Bullets were breaking windows, splintering wood off the corners of buildings, and whining through the air. MacLean put another robber out of action with a bullet through the shoulder. Then he had his face sprayed with splinters of rock as another slug struck the big chunk of ore. Doc calmly peered down the sights of his .303 and dropped a fourth bandit.

After that MacLean found he was out of ammunition. He made a dash across open ground to the general store, where the owner tossed him a box of cartridges. Another bullet clipped the wall above Doc's head as he scurried back to the big rock.

Two members of the outlaw gang were now dead and four others had been wounded. Two of them tried to get on a horse that was tied nearby, but they were too badly injured to manage it. The one robber who was still on his feet was Dzachot Bekuzaroff, still protected it seemed by whatever guardian devil had gotten him out of the Sakhalin labour camp. He made it to the bush, fired one last shot at the townsmen, then vanished into the trees. The four wounded Russians limped and dragged themselves after their leader.

As the gun smoke cleared, Bishop, Fenton, and Gaslin came out of the bank. An overanxious citizen thought they were more bandits and fired a blast from his shotgun. Fortunately, only Fenton was struck by a few pellets in the shoulder.

Two dead bandits lay where they had fallen. They were later identified as Obysel Borsaef and Mischa Merzakoff. New Hazelton's young policeman finally arrived, but having no experience in manhunts, he asked Doc MacLean to take charge of the posse that would pursue the rest of the gang. Before he led the other men into the bush, Doc gave Eva a shard of rock he had found on the brim of his hat. It was a piece of silver ore that an outlaw bullet had splintered off the rock, and he was keeping it as a souvenir.

Over the next two days the townsmen tracked down the four wounded bank robbers. One of them made the mistake of trying to shoot it out with Doc MacLean and got bullet wounds in his hand

Two outlaws slain in the New Hazelton gun battle lie where they fell on the wooden sidewalk. (British Columbia Archives B-01386)

and shoulder for his trouble. The leader, Bekuzaroff, escaped with the loot from the holdup — about $1,100. Three of the captured bandits were Zarachmet Kalaeff, Boris Manukoff, and Adeku Smajloff. The fourth man, Wano Dzntzoff, died of his wounds.

There was no solid evidence to tie this gang with the November robbery, so the prisoners couldn't be charged with the murder of Jock McQueen. The three were sentenced to twenty years each for armed robbery. Nonetheless, the people of New Hazelton were certain the two robberies had been committed by the same gang.

For Doc MacLean the excitement didn't end when the police took away the captives and the dead outlaws. In June the police in Vancouver sent word that a jailhouse informer had told them that a brother of one of the slain bandits was heading for New Hazelton to get revenge. There had been mention of a "tall priest with curly hair" — Doc MacLean! A description of the would-be avenger accompanied the message. Among other things, he was a tall, burly man with a big brown moustache.

A man of that description did indeed show up in New Hazelton. Doc MacLean met him on the street, hands on his hips and a gun belt strapped around his waist. If the man had come looking for trouble, he quickly changed his mind. The town constable questioned the stranger as to why he was in town. He didn't like the man's answers and told him to be on the next train out. The stranger left the next morning, escorted by a detective who made sure he didn't get off at the next stop.

The completion of railway construction meant the end of New Hazelton. In 1915 Doc MacLean moved his family to Quesnel. MacLean worked there and in other B.C. communities as a veterinarian, a preacher, and a schoolteacher. He died in 1975 at the age of ninety-five. His gunfight with the outlaws in 1914 made him a legend in British Columbia.

14 THE REID-DAVIS GANGS
Badmen on the Western Border

A decade before John Dillinger, Pretty Boy Floyd, Bonnie and Clyde, and other notorious "Automobile Bandits" of Depression-era America were capturing headlines with their lawless exploits, bankers in small towns in the American and Canadian West lived in dread of two men: John J. Reid and Arthur Davis. These men were the leaders of gangs that robbed banks with stunning regularity, made their escapes in powerful cars, and had the police on the lookout in five states and four provinces.

John J. Reid was born Leslie Ayer in Prince Rupert, British Columbia, in 1895. He was known to use many aliases, but he preferred Reid. His charming manner and his silver tongue earned him the nickname "Smiling Johnny." Trouble with the law began early in life for Smiling Johnny. He was in and out of jails throughout his teenage years and did prison time in Saskatchewan and Alberta for illegal possession of guns and explosives. On August 7, 1920, he was one of the lucky ones to obtain an early release from Edmonton Penitentiary in Alberta because the prison was being shut down. He went south, and sometime early in 1921 in Minot, North Dakota, he met thirty-three-year-old Arthur Davis.

American-born Davis had a criminal record dating back to 1910. His specialty was cracking safes. In criminal jargon he was a "soupman," an expert with explosives like nitroglycerine. Davis allegedly served with the American army during World War I and was embittered by the experience. He resumed his criminal career and was imprisoned for bank robbery. Davis had just been released on parole when he met Smiling Johnny Reid.

The two decided to pool their talents for a series of bank heists. Reid, the brains of the outfit, would do the planning while Davis would handle the "hot soup," or nitro. They would employ a long list of small-time punks and hoodlums as drivers, informants, muscle, and scouts. One of the last, whose job was to case prospective banks for the gang, was Davis's wife, Rhea. Reid was also married by this time, but his wife didn't participate in any robberies.

A Johnny Reid robbery was always well planned. Scouts and sometimes local informants tipped the gang off as to which small-town banks most likely had plenty of cash in the vaults and what the layout of the bank was. Reid also knew in advance if bank employees lived in backroom or upstairs premises (common at that time), and if the live-in clerk had a gun. The fact that small towns were isolated made them inviting targets. They usually had only one sheriff or con-

Edmonton Penitentiary in Alberta, once home to "Smiling Johnny" Reid. (Alberta Archives B4421)

stable, and communications with the outside world could be cut simply by snipping telegraph and telephone wires. That meant the bandits would be long gone by the time state or provincial police were informed of the robbery. If the robbers needed tools to force entry into a bank building or pry open a safe, they could find them in the railway shed near every small town's train station or in the local hardware store. All a bank burglar had to do to get the tools of the trade was kick down a door or smash a window.

The bandits would strike late at night or in the early morning. If a clerk was inside, they would tie him up "for his protection." A mixture of bread dough and nitro was used to blow the safe. Outside, armed men stood guard to warn off anyone awakened by the sound of the blast who might come snooping. Sometimes the gang even put a man in front of the local policeman's home to head the cop off if he had any ideas about being a hero. With the cash and bonds stuffed into grain sacks, the outlaws would pile into their car and head for the nearest state or provincial line or the international border. Because Reid and Davis made Minot their headquarters, they didn't rob banks in North Dakota.

The gang started with a spree of robberies in Montana, knocking over four banks between April 11 and August 20, 1921. Then, in September, they hit the banks in Homestead and Denton, Montana, and slipped across the state line to a hideout in Williston, North Dakota.

Someone tipped off the sheriff in Homestead that Davis had pulled the robbery in his town and then told the lawman where the thief was holed up. Montana and North Dakota police raided the hideout and found only Davis in the house. The rest of the gang members were out. Davis was packed off to Montana's Deer Lodge Penitentiary, firmly believing that Smiling Johnny had double-crossed him. But he didn't share his suspicions with Rhea, who visited him in prison and still ran with Reid's gang.

With Davis behind bars, Reid added two new members to his gang — James King and John Mahon, both of whom had long criminal records and used a variety of aliases. Mahon was on parole from Saskatchewan Penitentiary. On the night of March 27, 1922, the gang hit the Royal Bank in Ladner, British Columbia, and got away with $132,000 in cash and bonds. Gang members later said that

Canada was attractive to them because the police there weren't as trigger-happy as American cops. No doubt the criminals were well aware of the sorry state of western Canada's provincial police forces. World War I had severely depleted the ranks of the Royal Canadian Mounted Police, and to fill the gaps the western provinces had formed their own provincial police departments. However, poor funding left the officers under-equipped and in no position to deal with well-organized, highly mobile bandits like the Reid bunch.

After burying the loot from the Ladner robbery in Vancouver's Stanley Park, Reid lay low until May 24 when the gang struck the town of Lafleche, Saskatchewan. This time things didn't go well. Two blasts of nitro failed to open the safe, and the town constable was shot in the leg. The gang had to flee empty-handed. The robbers made up for this disappointment by hitting three Montana banks in June and two more in July. Then, on August 1, they tried their luck in Canada again, raiding the bank at MacGregor, Manitoba. Once again the vault proved to be too sturdy for the explosives, and the bandits departed with only the $25 they found in a cash drawer. The badmen ran into another stubborn vault when they tried to rob a bank at Carievale, Saskatchewan, on August 23.

A string of successes followed as the gang hit banks in Kilarney, Manitoba; Foremost, Alberta; and Glentana, Montana. After that the thieves headed back to Manitoba to the town of Melita. In the Glentana holdup a citizen who blundered onto the robbery scene was shot in the foot. Only now were police beginning to understand that one gang was responsible for the rash of bank burglaries. Soon they would have two gangs to worry about.

On September 22, through some bureaucratic error, Arthur Davis was paroled from prison. He didn't rejoin the Reid Gang, still believing Smiling Johnny had betrayed him. Instead he sent for Rhea, then formed his own gang. Among the criminals he recruited were three Canadians: Billy Coffron, Doc Walkup, and Roy Haugen. The new gang's first target was the Bank of Montreal in Ceylon, Saskatchewan, the hometown of the three Canuck bandits. They struck early in the morning of September 27 and made off with $23,000 in cash and securities. At about the same time, and in the same province, Reid and his boys were looting the Union Bank in Moosomin. Some of the men in that town heard that a robbery was in progress and went to the local armoury for weapons. But by the time they arrived at the bank the robbers were gone. The town's lone constable tried to go after the outlaws, but their fast Cadillac easily outdistanced his Ford.

The alarm was now spreading all along the international line. Not everything committed to the "safety" of a bank was insured. Some towns formed vigilance committees to protect their banks. The Saskatchewan Provincial Police armed officers in border communities with machine guns and made arrangements with civilians who owned fast cars to allow the police to use them in the event of a robbery. Plainclothes detectives were placed in banks considered to be likely targets. The Canadian Pacific Railway and rural telephone companies provided employees with signal rockets that were to be fired off if anyone found telephone or telegraph lines that had been cut. Almost as if he were thumbing his nose at these precautions, Reid plundered the bank in Fairfield, Montana, on October 17. Davis kept his hand in by knocking over the bank in Sheridan, Montana. The Montana and American Bankers associations responded by hiring the Burns Detective Agency.

The two gangs took a holiday for the winter, but in the spring of 1923 they were back on the road. On April 17, Davis and his boys struck the bank at Valier, Montana, and made a clean getaway ... almost! This time Davis himself left a clue. He unknowingly dropped a spare set of car keys in the bank, which were found after the robbery. The Burns detectives began the painstaking task of tracking the keys to a specific car — and an owner. A few weeks later Davis ran into more bad luck. His gang attempted a daylight raid on the bank in Gildford, Montana. This time they were thwarted by a gun-toting clerk. Roy Haugen had his chest grazed by a bullet. Deeming discretion the better part of valour, the bandits fled.

At about the same time in early May the Reid Gang blew the safe in the Bank of Montreal in Dollard, Saskatchewan, and got clean away. But there was tragedy in the wake of that robbery. A rumour circulated around town that two local boys, fifteen-year-old John Marquette and his fourteen-year-old brother, Emile, had seen the bandits and could identify one of them. One month later both boys drowned under mysterious circumstances. There was no evidence that the bank robbers had anything to do with the tragedy, but people wondered at the coincidence.

Then, on June 27, a pool-hall manager in Dollard was shot dead during a robbery. An American resident of the town, Fred Huss, was charged with murder, tried, and sentenced to hang. Before going to the gallows on February 22, 1924, Huss confessed that he had been a local informant for the Reid Gang in the bank robbery.

Meanwhile, the marauders were hard at it. On May 17, Smiling Johnny and his crew robbed the Bank of Toronto in Mather, Manitoba. Later that month the Davis outfit made midnight withdrawals from two more Montana banks. Then they gave Utah a taste of what Montana had been experiencing by robbing six banks in that state within a few weeks. Both gangs then made return visits to beleaguered Montana. The Davis boys plundered three more banks successfully, but when bandits believed to be the Reid Gang made an attempt on the bank in Hall, Montana, they got into a shootout with a storekeeper who was investigating a noise. Nobody was hurt in the exchange of shots, and the bandits made good their escape, but with no swag. The Reid Gang was also suspected in a raid on the Bank of Montreal in Greenwood, British Columbia, on October 17. Once again the thieves were disturbed before they could crack the safe, and sped out of town after one of them took a potshot at a man who had been roused by a noise.

In the meantime the Burns Detective Agency traced the owner of the car keys found at the Valier Bank the previous April. They belonged to Arthur Davis, who was on parole and had a house in Havre, Montana, where he was supposed to be honestly employed by a rancher named Ed Marshall. Police raided the house, but Davis was tipped off. Both he and Rhea were gone.

Now it was Smiling Johnny Reid's turn to make a mistake. On November 6 his gang hit the bank of Fairfield, Montana, a second time. The robbers found that the vault doors had been reinforced. They tried to cut through with an acetylene torch, but it was no use. When they left, the usually careful Reid forgot an acetylene tank. The police found the cylinder the next morning, and the Burns detectives began the hunt for its origin.

Davis was on the run now, since the police had evidence connecting him with at least one robbery, but he decided he had to make another score. On November 10 his bunch cleaned out a bank in Salesville, Montana. But this would be the gang's last job. Roy

Haugen wasn't happy with his share of the spoils from one of the robberies. He had been given a stack of stolen bonds that were a type difficult to unload for hard cash, and he had been sulking about it for months. Now he decided to turn stool pigeon. Since the cops were onto Davis, he thought, it just might be a matter of time before everyone was on the wanted list. So Haugen figured he better cut his losses while he had the chance. He contacted Walter S. Gordon of the Burns Detective Agency and made a deal. Haugen would tell Gordon all he wanted to know about the Davis Gang in return for leniency in court and a reward of $1,000 for every bandit Haugen's testimony helped to convict. That could potentially mean a lot of money, because the robberies had involved dozens of underworld characters.

Within days the police rounded up Billy Coffron, Doc Walkup, Rhea Davis, and several small-time hoodlums. Ed Marshall and a few Montana businessmen were arrested, as well. They had been instrumental in converting stolen bonds into cash. Many of the people arrested were in possession of both Canadian and American bonds, and in her purse Rhea had the plans for the gang's next bank robbery. In a gang hideout in Salt Lake City, the police found guns, burglar tools, and large quantities of nitroglycerine. Most of the loot was unaccounted for, and they still didn't have Arthur Davis. He was finally captured on December 13 in Stockton, California, by detectives acting on a tip. Squealers seem to have been the curse of Arthur Davis's life.

The acetylene canister found at the Fairfield bank was traced to a store in Seattle, Washington. The dealer there remembered selling it to a man whose description fitted that of a Canadian thief the detectives knew as Smiling Johnny Reid. The police decided to concentrate the search in the Seattle area. One day after Davis was picked up in California, Reid was arrested in the town of Renton, a few miles from Seattle, while mailing a letter in the post office.

Arthur Davis pleaded guilty to the Valier robbery and was sentenced to fifteen to thirty years. He told a reporter to pass on a message to young people: "The game doesn't pay — work for a living." Davis's wife, Rhea, was also sent to jail, but was found to be terminally ill. She was released on April 3, 1924, and died soon after.

Other gang members received long or short prison terms, depending on what kind of evidence the prosecution had and how sharp the defence lawyers were. In return for selling out his partners, Roy Haugen drew three to ten years, which meant he would be eligible for parole after eighteen months.

Even though John Reid and his buddies James King and John Mahon had robbed banks in the United States, the American authorities were convinced their Canadian counterparts had a stronger case against the trio and allowed them to be extradited to Canada. King and Mahon landed in the penitentiary at Prince Albert, Saskatchewan, but not Reid. There was wile behind Johnny's smile.

Many things were unusual about the Roaring Twenties, but few were more bizarre than Canada's "Cross of Gold" policy concerning robbers. In the years following World War I, many bank robberies in Canada were committed by veterans returning from the trenches of France to unemployment and hard times. There was a lot of public sympathy for these men, who were seen more as Robin Hoods than as hardened criminals. The Canadian Bankers Association decided that when such men were apprehended, if they returned the stolen money, or most of it, the banks wouldn't press charges. Nor would they oppose early parole if the man had to do prison time. This became known as the Cross of Gold policy because, according to Canadian historian Frank W. Anderson, whose book *The Border Bank Bandits* is the definitive study of the Reid-Davis gangs, if the robber didn't return the money, he was "crucified on a Cross of Gold."

John Reid wasn't a returned soldier from World War I, but he switched on the famous charm and went to work on the sentiment behind the policy. Between them, the Reid and Davis gangs had removed more than $2 million in cash and bonds from banks, an incredible sum in the 1920s. Smiling Johnny told the Canadian authorities he realized he had made a mistake. He had been led astray by bad companions and was now determined to reform himself and go straight. Reid had stolen bonds hidden in various locations, and as an act of good faith he said he would be glad to show the police where they were. The bank robber took the authorities to locations in Montana, North Dakota, Minnesota, Saskatchewan, Manitoba, and Vancouver's Stanley Park, where they retrieved hundreds of thousands of dollars in bonds and securities. The banks, of course, were delighted to get these valuable documents back. Reid assured one and all that he was truly sorry for the bad things he had done and would never do them again. The law chastised him with a two-year suspended sentence. Johnny Reid, one of the most notorious Canadian desperadoes of the 1920s, was still smiling.

15
McFadden and Hotrum
The Only Men in the Wide, Wide World

At 9:00 p.m. on Saturday, March 5, 1921, Toronto taxi driver Walter Hulse picked up three men at the corner of Queen and Peter streets. These were no ordinary fares out for a night at a speakeasy or a dance hall. John "Jack" Conley, nineteen, and William "Mac" McFadden, thirty-two, were both veterans of World War I, while Roy "Patsy" Hotrum, twenty-two, was an ex-con and sometime amateur boxer. All three were bandits, or *yeggmen*, in the street slang of the time.

Along with young Conley's uncle, Arthur Conley, a hard case with a long record of robberies and prison terms, the gang had been responsible for a rash of armed holdups in Toronto and Hamilton, knocking over drugstores and butcher shops for paltry amounts of cash. For whatever reason, Uncle Arthur wasn't along for this job. Hulse would later tell police that the gang often hired him as a driver but that he was unaware they were engaged in robbery. According to other testimony, Hulse not only knew what his passengers were up to, but helped to select the targets and shared in the loot. It helped pay for his car.

On this Saturday night they were heading for Hamilton, Hotrum's hometown, to rob a butcher shop. The gang of small-time hoodlums seemed partial to butcher shops, perhaps because McFadden had been a butcher. At least that was what he had entered as his occupation on his recruitment form when he joined the Canadian army in his hometown of London in 1917.

The quartet left Toronto and drove a short distance along the Hamilton highway, but the fog was so bad that they decided to turn around and go back. Hotrum later claimed he told the others: "Let's call it a night" and "You may think I'm yellow, but I'm going home." Someone evidently changed his mind, because soon they were cruising Toronto streets looking for another place to rob. Hulse wanted them to stick up a garage owner who supposedly owed him money, and possibly they did beat up and rob a garage man that night. But whether they did or not, the evening was still young. The thieves stopped in front of a butcher shop on Dupont Street, but there were customers in the store. Then they drove on to another butcher shop on Avenue Road and found the same problem.

At that point they might have been willing to give it up as a poor night for larceny, but someone in the car said, "Go down Manning." As they passed Sabine's Drugstore at the corner of Manning Avenue and Harbord Street, someone said, "There's the store!" Hulse parked the car around the corner on Euclid Avenue but kept the motor running. Conley opted to remain in the car with the driver, because he was known in the neighbourhood and was afraid he would be recognized.

McFadden and Hotrum got out and walked to Sabine's Drugstore. Peeking inside, they saw a customer at the counter, so they walked down the street a little way and then came back. This time they saw only the pharmacist in the store. Exactly what happened after that would prove to be a perplexing question for the Toronto Police Department's investigators and for the prosecuting and defence attorneys in the subsequent trials.

It was ten minutes before his 11:00 p.m. closing time, and pharmacist Leonard Cecil Sabine was counting out the day's receipts. There was some cash on the counter, some still in the till, and he had just put a little over $40 in his pocket. He looked up and saw two young men enter the store. The lower parts of their faces were masked with handkerchiefs. One of them approached him, brandishing a revolver with a long black barrel. "Throw up your hands!" the bandit ordered.

Young Sabine had allegedly once said he would never willingly surrender to robbers, but on this occasion he didn't take the threat seriously. "Cut out your fooling," he said.

In the backroom of the pharmacy Sabine's employee, William Stokes, heard the sounds of a scuffle and then a shot. The clerk looked out through a peephole and spied a man of about five feet, seven or eight inches, wearing a dark coat and a cap, with a white handkerchief around his lower face. The man was holding a smoking long-barrelled revolver. Stokes didn't see a second man, but he heard someone, not Sabine, shout, "Cut it out! Cut it out!" The man scooped up some money from the counter and fled the store. When Stokes hurried out from the backroom, he found Sabine unconscious on the floor, blood oozing from a bullet hole in his stomach.

Around the corner on Euclid Avenue McFadden and Hotrum piled into the waiting getaway car and told Hulse, "Beat it! Make it fast! The dicks will be around!" Asked how much they had taken, one of the robbers replied, "Nothing! I had to plug him to get away." Hulse sped off into the night, dropping McFadden somewhere because Mac desperately needed to get a drink.

Sabine was rushed to Toronto Western Hospital. He regained consciousness long enough to tell police, "Two men came in and held me up." Sabine described the man in the dark coat as the one who had shot him with the long black gun. The other man, Sabine said, stood at the door and didn't participate in the robbery. Sabine said his attacker had a dark complexion and thin features. He also said, "He grinned and drew his lips up. He had a devilish-looking appearance — a horrible appearance." Had the pharmacist managed to unmask the bandit momentarily before he was shot?

Dr. F.R. Scott, the surgeon attending to Sabine, told him, "Things might not be as bad as they look."

"I hope you're right," Sabine replied.

The pharmacist underwent surgery, but at 1:20 on Sunday afternoon he died. The doctors removed a .38 calibre bullet from his body. They said the damage the slug had done would have made recovery almost impossible. Sabine left behind a wife but no children. In their haste to get away, the bandits had taken a grand total of $35, leaving the money in the till and the cash in Sabine's pocket.

The manhunt was on as Toronto seethed with outrage. There was evidence that the men who had killed Sabine were the same criminals who had pulled other armed robberies in the city, but the police didn't have much to go on. It was the gangsters themselves who gave the police the break they needed, and they didn't wait long to do it.

Most other criminals, if faced with almost certain murder charges, would have lain low for a while or slipped off to parts far away. But brains didn't seem to figure largely in the makeup of this gang. On Monday, March 7, with L.C. Sabine not yet even in the ground, Jack and Arthur Conley, Patsy Hotrum, and faithful driver Walter Hulse made that overdue trip to Hamilton, not to stick up a butcher shop, but to knock over Rousseau's Jewellery Store for $1,000 worth of merchandise. Not a bad haul in 1921 currency! They also took a revolver they found behind the counter. No one was hurt, but the thieves left clerk George Brown bound and gagged. They hightailed it back to Toronto and quickly fenced their loot that very afternoon. Then, incredibly, they went off to do another stickup. At about 5:00 p.m. they parked on Britain Street. Hulse, as usual, stayed in the car with the engine running. John Conley and his Uncle Arthur went around the corner to Ammon Davis's jewellery store at 176 Queen Street East. They drew their guns and said, "Hands up!"

Showing more courage than common sense, especially in the wake of the Sabine murder, Ammon Davis tried to tackle one of the Conleys. Davis was luckier than Sabine. Instead of shooting him the other Conley struck him on the head with the butt of his gun. Davis would later make a statement that the gun had a long black barrel, but his evidence was ruled inadmissible in court.

The noise of the struggle brought Davis's two sons running from the backroom. The robbers fled empty-handed, and Davis and his boys went after them. As the pursuers turned onto Britain Street, they saw the bandits climb into a car. One of the hoodlums turned and fired a shot that didn't hit anyone. Then the getaway car sped away. But bystanders had noted the make of the car and had taken down the licence number. An hour later the police arrested Walter Hulse, who made a deal to escape prosecution. He told the police where they could find the Conleys, McFadden, and Hotrum. The officers were advised that the men they were after were highly dangerous and that they should be prepared to shoot the bandits on sight.

The constables found McFadden in bed in his rooming house on Pembroke Street. When the policemen burst through the door with weapons drawn, McFadden threw his arms in the air and cried, "My hands are up!" The Conleys and Hotrum were captured just as easily in a raid on a house on Markham Street. Guns were found on the suspects' premises, including a nickel-plated .32 revolver and the pistol that had been taken from the Hamilton jewellery store. But none of the seized weapons could have fired the bullet that killed Sabine. Nor did they match the long black gun described by Sabine and Stokes. But McFadden's landlady said that she had once seen a gun like that in a partially opened drawer in his room. And among the ammunition the police found in the Conleys' rooms were some .38 calibre cartridges of the same manufacture as the bullet taken from Sabine's body. The police had little doubt that one of the men now in custody had gunned down the pharmacist. But who had actually pulled the trigger?

In the investigation and the May trials that followed the arrests, it became clear that Arthur Conley hadn't been along on the drugstore heist, but he would get fifteen years in prison for armed robbery, anyway. Jack Conley had been in on the drugstore job but had remained in the car. He drew a twenty-year sentence and would keep his uncle company in Kingston and then some. Roy Hotrum and William McFadden both admitted going to Sabine's Drugstore, but their stories clashed. Each accused the other of being the shooter. They were tried separately and appeared as witnesses against each other. Each had supporting testimony from other gang members.

Hotrum claimed that on the fateful Saturday night McFadden had been drinking and was edgy. He said that when they got out of the car on Euclid Avenue he himself didn't have a gun, so he borrowed an unloaded nickel-plated .32 revolver from Conley. Hotrum insisted that Mac had "a bigger gun" than he had. Conley, too, said he had given his .32 to Patsy and that Mac had a gun with a long gunmetal-blue barrel — a .38 or a .45.

McFadden denied all of this. He said he hadn't been drinking and that it was *he* who had borrowed the .32 from Conley, while Patsy carried the bigger gun. Hulse backed him up in this. "Jack [Conley] says to McFadden, 'Have you got a gun, Mac?' And McFadden said that he hadn't."

A man named Bert Malone testified that Hulse had spoken to him in the jail infirmary and that Hulse had said he wasn't going to see McFadden hanged. Hulse denied saying any such thing.

Hotrum testified that when they got to the door of the store McFadden said, "We'll have to go in and make this store fast." He said he told Mac to take his time and not to shoot. Then, he continued, "Mac said, 'Let's go.'" Hotrum said they entered the store, and while he stayed back to guard the door, Mac advanced on Sabine quickly.

"He must have surprised Mr. Sabine," Hotrum told the court. "Just as I got to the door I could see them both. Mac was in the passageway at the end of the counter and Mr. Sabine seemed to be backed into a corner. It looked as if there was going to be a fight. I had just reached the door on the right-hand side. I hollered to them to cut it out. It seemed as if Mr. Sabine was going to grab Mac. Then there was a shot. I beat it."

Again McFadden told a different tale. He testified that when they got to the door "I said I wasn't going in. Patsy said, 'You're yellow,' and then he darted in. Patsy stopped just before he got to the counter. I saw him put his hand in his right overcoat pocket, and he had a gun when he pulled his hand out. It was a big black gun. I hollered, 'Cut it out! Cut it out!' He fired and I saw the man drop. He came out and caught up to me at the corner of the store. I said, 'For God's sake, what did you do that for?' Patsy said, 'I had to punch him to get away.'"

The discrepancies continued over who had said what as they sped away in their car. According to Conley, McFadden said, "I had to plug him to get away. I asked Mac where he had hit him. He said, 'In the leg.' I think it was at that time that Hotrum gave me back my gun."

However, Hulse claimed Hotrum said he had "punched a man in the stomach." Hulse insisted he didn't know at the time that Hotrum meant Sabine had been shot. McFadden's attorney was quick to point out that "punch in the stomach" was an expression a boxer would use.

There were other conflicting points for the jury to deliberate. Sabine had told police that two men entered his shop, but McFadden said he never entered the store. Stokes had seen only one man. The facial description Sabine had given the police fitted McFadden more than it did Hotrum, but the dark coat he described was more like the one Hotrum had been wearing. And how reliable were statements made by a man in his death agony?

Then there were the backgrounds of the two men. McFadden

came from a respectable London family, and aside from a few charges of public drunkenness, he had only one charge of petty theft on his record. He had never spent time in jail and had served with the Canadian army overseas during World War I. His former commanding officer, appearing as a character witness, said that McFadden had been a good soldier and had never been in trouble. When McFadden returned to Canada after the war, he went to work as a butcher in Winnipeg but then lost his job. He drifted to Toronto where he was forced to go on "city relief" — welfare.

Roy Hotrum had been in trouble with the law since 1910 when he was sent to reform school at the age of eleven. He came from a family of eighteen children and was the only one to have problems with the police. His father, who appeared as a character witness, said that Roy was a good boy, but admitted "he would steal." At the time that William McFadden was off serving his country, Roy Hotrum was in prison.

Throughout the trials McFadden seemed to keep his composure, while Hotrum at times was seen to weep. At one point Hotrum's legal counsel, W.K. Murphy, said to McFadden, "It is between you two. You are the only men in the wide, wide world who know who shot Sabine."

Nevertheless, the men stuck to their stories and wouldn't budge, even under the most harrowing cross-examination. Hotrum was the first to be tried, and the jury found him guilty. Justice Kelly reserved passing sentence until after McFadden's trial but said that in his opinion, based on the evidence, it was Hotrum who had fired the fatal shot. Still, that didn't mean McFadden was off the hook. As the justice explained to the court, when two or more armed men commit an unlawful act, they demonstrate a willingness to commit murder and all involved are responsible and answerable to the law for any violent act that ensues.

McFadden was tried by a different judge and a different jury, and he, too, was found guilty. Justice Logie stated that he also believed that Hotrum had pulled the trigger but that both men were equally guilty. He sentenced McFadden to be hanged on August 3, 1921. Two days later Justice Kelly passed the same sentence on Hotrum. In the prisoner's dock Mac turned to Patsy and said, "I guess you are going to get it, too."

The attorneys for both condemned men filed appeals, but the sentences were upheld. En route to Kingston Penitentiary, Jack Conley changed his tune. He told the press that at the trial he thought he had been telling the truth, but now he believed Hotrum was the killer. Arthur Conley said that he had owned the .38 calibre long-barrelled revolver and had destroyed it. On May 26 a Toronto City Hall guard submitted a signed affidavit stating that Hotrum had told him McFadden didn't shoot Sabine. A day later Hotrum denied making the statement. "What I did say was that I hoped McFadden would get off so that he might tell the truth about me."

Despite public outrage over the murder, sympathy began to well up for McFadden. Six members of the jury that had convicted him signed a petition for executive clemency which, if acted on, would see the death sentence commuted to life imprisonment. By the first of July, 2,000 people in Toronto and another 2,000 in London added their names to those of the jurors. In Hamilton more than 7,000 signed a similar document hoping to save Hotrum from the noose. Spokesmen for the Great War Veterans Association added their voices to the appeal for McFadden, but the Belleville chapter of that organization protested. Their first duty, they said, was to uphold the law of the land. The government shared that view, and the pleas for mercy fell on deaf ears.

Nonetheless, there was considerable speculation that if one of the condemned men confessed to the shooting, the other might get a last-minute stay of execution. Two days before the scheduled date of the hanging, people waited anxiously for the real killer to come clean. The government insisted that both men would hang regardless of who had actually fired the gun, but as the hours crept by anticipation mounted. McFadden told his mother and sister that he was still hopeful. On August 2 the Salvation Army chaplain attending to the doomed men sent a telegraph to the minister of justice stating that he and everyone on the jail staff were convinced that Hotrum had done the deed.

But there was no confession.

At eight o'clock on the morning of August 3, 1921, William McFadden and Roy Hotrum stood facing each other on the gallows of the Don Jail. They were equally guilty in the eyes of the law. But in each other's eyes? Which one knew that the last thing he would see on earth was the face of a killer? The hoods were pulled over their heads, the nooses adjusted, and the trap sprung. "No confession was forthcoming from either," the newspapers reported.

16 THE MURRELL GANG
Taught to Kill

*I*n the spring of 1921, William Murrell, Sr., didn't know what to do about his sons William, Jr., and Sidney, age twenty-five and twenty-six. Murrell had brought his family to Canada from England twelve years earlier and had settled in a house in London, Ontario. Within a few years Bill and Sid, the eldest of six children, were getting into trouble with the police over petty thefts. When World War I began, Murrell went overseas to fight. Bill and Sid, though mere lads, also joined up. Bill was in France, while Sid served in a Royal Navy submarine.

Murrell returned home from the war a bitter man with leanings towards socialism. Bill and Sid had come out of the war alive but were bent on raising hell. They covered their arms and chests with tattoos and soon made themselves well-known to the London police. They were wild and beyond their parents' control.

Early in 1920, Bill punched his mother, Mabel, on the jaw. His father had the police on him for that, and Bill did thirty days in the slammer. The jail time didn't bother the young man. He often said he would rather go to jail than work, because in jail a man got three square meals a day and a warm place to sleep and didn't have to lift a finger for any of it. But upon his release Bill didn't return home, and his parents had no contact with him for more than a year. When they finally did see him again, it was under the worst of circumstances.

Still living at home, Sid gave no explanation about what he did when he went out at night. When his father asked, Sid would reply, "What's worrying you, old-timer? I'm old enough to take care of myself."

Sid had a German revolver he had brought home from the war. His parents didn't know that a friend had offered to buy the gun, but Sid had refused to sell it, telling the man the weapon was "my living." Bill, Sid, and a few pals were, in fact, responsible for a crime wave that hit London and nearby communities, pulling at least a dozen burglaries and several stickups. They had even looted an express car at London's Grand Trunk Railway station. Just a few nights before the crime that would make their names known across the country, Sid and Bill robbed a Chinese laundry in London. The brothers struck down the two proprietors with the butts of their revolvers, then kicked the men mercilessly as they lay helpless on the floor. That job netted the Murrell boys $30.

In April a friend told the Murrells that the Home Bank in Melbourne, a small community southwest of London, would be easy pickings. There were "only a pair of janes" in the bank the informant said and the village had no constable. In the early morning of April 11, the Murrell brothers, Henry "Slim" Williams, and Pat Norton climbed into a stolen McLaughlin sedan and headed down the highway to Melbourne. Along the way an argument broke out in the car. Williams had no qualms about going for a joyride in a stolen car, but it wasn't until they were on the road that the others told him they were going to rob a bank. Williams wanted out. Norton told him to do what he was told or "I'll drill you!"

They sped through Melbourne at about 5:00 a.m. Bill complained that Sid was driving too fast. He said he "couldn't get an eyeful" of the Home Bank. They pulled over at a farm a few miles out of town, where they built a fire and cooked some breakfast. Then they passed around a bottle for a few belts of liquid courage. The farmer who owned the property came down and asked them what they were doing. The boys said they were waiting to meet a man who was going to sell them some bootleg whiskey. They lazed around their campfire until 10:30, then got into the car for the drive back to Melbourne. Slim Williams was still against the whole thing, but he was afraid of Norton.

Shortly before 11:00, Home Bank manager R.E. McCandles was in the teller's cage talking to Agnes Campbell, one of the "janes." The other woman, Irma Wright, was just going out the front door. As she stepped outside, four men entered the bank. She saw that three of them had guns. Williams, who was unarmed, had been told to stay at the door to stop anyone from entering or leaving. But he went into the bank with the others and didn't attempt to detain Irma Wright.

Wright immediately ran into the store next door and called the village telephone exchange. Within moments the operator was telephoning the alarm to businesses throughout the community. The first place she called was Campbell Brothers' Garage. (The proprietors weren't related to Agnes Campbell.)

Inside the Home Bank, Norton ordered McCandles and Agnes to put up their hands. Instead, Agnes dashed to slam the vault door shut. Norton and Bill Murrell went behind the counter and told McCandles to open it. When he refused, they pistol-whipped him. Agnes ran out the back door. The robbers didn't try to stop her because, as one of them later explained, they didn't know how to deal with a woman. She ran across the road to the Union Bank and told manager E.B. Teacker that the Home Bank was being robbed.

When brothers Robert, Russell, and Stuart Campbell, garage owners, received the phone call, they grabbed some tools and headed straight for the Home Bank, which was a short distance down the road. Stuart dashed into a hardware store and came out with a .22 calibre rifle, for which he had no bullets. As they approached the bank, Russell, a veteran of World War I, posted himself at the opening of an alley that ran alongside the building to block that avenue of escape.

Robert and Stuart entered the front door and saw two men standing just inside. Two others were behind the counter. Stuart raised the empty rifle and told them to put their hands up. One bandit, Sid Murrell, bolted out the side door that led to the alley. Norton and Bill Murrell opened fire with their revolvers, but they were either poor shots or they weren't trying to hit anyone, because neither Stuart nor Robert was hurt.

In the alley Sid ran into Russell Campbell, who grappled with him as Robert emerged from the side door. For a few seconds the two men scuffled. Then the thunder of two gunshots rang down the alleyway. One bullet grazed Campbell's leg. The other bullet punched into his body just below the left armpit and travelled all the way through, severing an aorta and stopping just as it bulged the skin on Campbell's right side. Thirty-three-year-old Russell Campbell, who had survived three years in the trenches of France, was dead before he hit the ground.

Now Sid Murrell saw Robert Campbell coming after him and took a shot at the man. Robert ducked behind a stairway. Sid made a dash to escape the alleyway, but Robert and Stuart tackled him and brought him down. They were quickly assisted by other men who had come running as soon as they heard about the robbery. One was E.B. Teacker, who had come out of his bank armed with two revolvers.

While everyone was distracted by the fracas at the end of the alleyway, Slim Williams, the man who had wanted no part of the robbery, burst out the front door and ran down the street, clutching a valise containing $1,500 he had scooped out of the cash drawers. Teacker raised one of his guns and fired, hitting Williams in the hand. Williams stopped, dropped the valise, and cried, "I'm through!"

By now a crowd had gathered in front of the bank — men armed with rifles, shotguns, and even pitchforks. There was no lock-up in Melbourne, so they tied Sid Murrell and Slim Williams to a telephone pole. A friend of the slain man struck one of the bandits. Stuart Campbell growled at Sid, "You killed my brother!"

William Murrell (left) and Sid Murrell (beside him) in police custody after the attempted bank robbery in Melbourne, Ontario. (Glencoe and District Historical Society and JoAnn Galbraith)

"I'm not denying it," Sid replied, but it was said in more of a whine than in a tone of defiance.

Then someone said there had been four bandits. The crowd spread out to search the village. In a barn behind the Home Bank, an Oneida named Wilfrid Danford found Bill Murrell trying to hide in the hayloft. Murrell had tossed away his gun. Now he begged Danford not to shoot him. Danford seized the outlaw and threw him out the open loft door to a group of men waiting below. They hauled Bill to the main street and tied him up with the other two. Bill saw Campbell's body lying in a pool of blood. He whispered to Sid, "Did you shoot him?"

Sid replied, "Yes."

Bill snarled, "You fool!"

The fourth bandit, Pat Norton, managed to escape from the village into the woods.

An angry mob now surrounded the trussed-up bandits, and some citizens muttered about taking the law into their own hands. But police officers arrived from London to escort the Murrells and Williams into custody. There weren't enough constables to hunt for Norton, so they took the prisoners back to London.

For the next few days police and civilian volunteers trudged through woods and swamps looking for Norton. They found shacks in sugar bushes where the fugitive had evidently slept and eaten eggs pilfered from henhouses. One farm family reported that a strange man had forced them at gunpoint to provide him with food and had made such dire threats that after he left they had been afraid to go to the police. Officers watched the roads and railways, but Pat Norton had made a clean getaway.

In the London jail the Murrell brothers were anything but contrite. As Russell Campbell was buried with full military honours, they seemed to enjoy all the attention they were getting from police and the press. They even boasted of earlier robberies. Police soon had them connected to stickups in London, Hamilton, and Brantford. Police officers searched the Murrell home and found property stolen from a theatre in which Sid had worked as an usher. In the well behind the house they discovered the money boxes from the Grand Trunk express robbery. The boys' father helped the officers haul the evidence to the surface. William

Murrell, Sr., was grimly philosophic about his family's public humiliation. He blamed it on the war:

> *The government taught us to kill, and now it comes easy to those boys to shoot. I can't trust myself with a gun, or I would have used it a thousand times since I came home. There is nothing for the poor man but work, work, work. Go out and buy something for a dollar and sell it to the working man for $5. That is within the law. But steal any other way and you can't get away with it. They [his sons] might have known they couldn't fight the law, but they are game. They won't squeal, no matter what happens. The law can do anything to them, even hang them, but they have seen worse in the war.*

William Murrell was wrong when he said his boys wouldn't squeal. Sid and Bill readily gave the police Pat Norton's name. They even volunteered the information that he was from Hamilton. Detectives found Norton's wife working as a housekeeper on a farm near Hamilton. She told them Norton was the fourth bandit they were looking for and that she had left him because of his criminal ways. Norton had actually shown up at the farm with a couple of his hoodlum friends and had made her cook them a meal.

On April 21 the Murrells and Williams were taken back to Melbourne for a preliminary hearing. They almost didn't make it. Their car swerved on the highway and flipped over. The prisoners and their police escort crawled out of the wreck bruised but otherwise unhurt.

The Melbourne hall in which the inquiry was held was filled to capacity. So many local residents crowded into the room that part of the wooden floor collapsed, causing many people to run out in panic. When proceedings finally got underway, a magistrate committed all three prisoners to be tried for murder.

The trio's lawyer, J.M. Donahue, argued that all three men couldn't be tried for a crime committed by only one. The judge replied that they didn't have a leg to stand on. Sid Murrell lit a cigarette and told his companions to "cheer up."

The Murrell family was in the hall, and one of the boys' sisters suddenly ran up and hugged her brothers. Mabel Murrell sat and cried into a handkerchief. It was a touching scene, but outside the hall things started to turn ugly.

A large crowd jammed the area between the meeting hall and the police car. As policemen and the prisoners shouldered their way through, someone shouted they should get some rope and save the hangman a job. Other voices muttered in agreement. The Murrell girl tried to get close to her brothers, but someone shoved her back. Sid saw it and yelled, "Say, guy, quit your pushing there!"

A young man replied, "That's all right. *Your* pushing days are over!"

The officers finally bundled the three bandits into the car and drove back to London.

For the next few days the prisoners behaved as if everything were a big game. They sang noisy songs. They held a mock trial in their cell, followed by a mock hanging. When a visiting clergyman asked if they believed in hell, one of the Murrells answered, "Sure. It is down in Kingston and we'd as soon be hanged as go there." On May 2 the brothers set fire to their cell in what appeared to be a botched escape attempt.

After that the prisoners seemed to resign themselves to waiting for their trial in the fall assizes. The Murrells' mother and sisters were frequent visitors, and they often brought the boys home-cooked meals as a break from jailhouse fare. Another visitor was a young woman whose name wasn't recorded but who was described in the press as the wife of a war vet whose husband had left her when he learned she had been having an affair with Sid Murrell.

As the weeks following the cell fire passed with no further shenanigans, security at the Middlesex County jail became lax. On September 1, Sid's girlfriend visited the jail and sat talking to him through the bars for a long time. A turnkey overheard her say, "What is the matter, Sid? Have you lost your strength? Are you going to sit here till they hang you? Be a man!"

The turnkey didn't think anything of it. He should have. Twenty-four hours later the Murrell brothers were gone!

At 8:00 p.m. on September 2 a turnkey found the Murrells' cell empty. He was the first jail employee to check on the cell in over an hour, which meant the escapees had a good start. They had sawn through the bars of their window. A construction crew that had been doing some work in the jail yard had carelessly left a ladder at the work site. The Murrells had used it to scale the wall.

In the empty cell the guards found a six-inch hacksaw blade with an improvised grip made from the flush handle of a toilet fastened with chewing gum and electrical tape. The brothers had evidently been at work on the bars for quite some time, using black soap to fill in the cut marks when they weren't sawing. The guards also discovered a note that said: "Goodbye. Good luck. God bless you all."

The Murrells had certainly had outside help, and police had no doubt that a car had been waiting for them on the other side of the wall. Nonetheless, the slackness of security in the jail drew harsh criticism from the press. There was a major shakeup of personnel at the jail — from the governor's office down to the turnkeys.

The situation became even more embarrassing when news got out that the Murrells had been seen in Woodstock within hours of the jailbreak. They had been driving a high-powered car and had stopped to buy some road maps and ask for directions to Niagara Falls. Woodstock police weren't aware of the escape, didn't hear about it, in fact, for thirteen hours after it occurred.

There was more. In their flight the brothers stopped to mail a letter to the press. The text of the letter, written by the same hand that had scrawled the note found in the Murrells' cell, said in poorly spelled and ungrammatical English:

Just a few lines to the press. As know doubt you will all be looking for some news after our wonderful escape. Well, we found it quite a joy to have the pleasure of the good air that we have mist for quite a long time. But while I am droping you these few lines I must say that the London plice are very slow, as it was only 20 minutes after we was out we passed 4 plicemen and I think it is time the poor boobs wake up, as they dont seem to know any one that is had a wash and shave and they always have a lot to bost about, but we dont see it. I will let you know more later on as we feel to good to write very much at present. So hop you will excuse this short note and wish us the best of luck the same as many others. We remain yours truly. THE BOYS.

The police searched everywhere, followed up every lead, and posted a $3,000 reward. Nothing! The Murrells had vanished as effectively as the elusive Pat Norton, of whom the law had found no trace. The police didn't even have Norton's fingerprints on file. In mid-October armed bandits held up banks in Hamilton and Wyoming, Ontario, within days of each other. Police suspected that the Murrells, in need of "getaway money," were involved.

The London police sent information on the Murrells, including their fingerprints, to police departments all over Canada and the United States. They assured the public that the "Boys" would soon be back behind bars. Meanwhile, Slim Williams, who had been in a separate cell from the busy Murrells, was convicted of armed robbery and sentenced to eight years in Kingston. He still had a murder charge hanging over him but couldn't be tried until at least one of his colleagues was apprehended. It might take some time, but the police and the courts were patient.

Almost a year and nine months after the jailbreak, London police received the news they had been waiting for. In May 1923, Sidney Murrell had been arrested in Susanville, a town in Northern California near the Nevada border. The local sheriff, a man named Carter, had caught him driving a stolen car. Sheriff Carter checked the prisoner's fingerprints and found they matched those of a man wanted for bank robbery and murder in Canada and who had a $3,000 reward on his head. The irony of it all was that Sid had purchased the car, unaware it had been stolen! A man arrested with Murrell was at first thought to be Pat Norton but was soon identified as someone else.

Sid tried to make a break from the Susanville jail, but Sheriff Carter wasn't about to let the reward slip through his fingers. He thwarted the escape attempt, then shipped Murrell off to San Francisco to be locked up in the more secure jail there. San Francisco police officers kept a close watch on their Canadian prisoner, because they had heard rumours that Bill Murrell and Pat Norton were in the vicinity and would try to bust Sid out. However, if the two outlaws were in San Francisco, they made no attempt to spring Sid.

When the extradition proceedings were completed, Ontario Provincial Police officers travelled to California and took Murrell back to Ontario by train, handcuffed and in leg irons. By July 22 he was in London in a jail with beefed-up security. He wasn't allowed visitors. Guards kept him under twenty-four-hour surveillance.

At first Sid told reporters he hadn't seen Bill since the night of the breakout. Then he spun a colourful yarn in which the brothers hopped a freight train to Halifax and got jobs on a ship. The pair went to the West Indies and then to Mexico, where they jumped ship and travelled overland to the United States. They wandered around, making their money, he said, by gambling. Of course, he said he didn't know where either Bill or Pat Norton were.

Murrell denied shooting Russell Campbell. He said he fired some shots in Melbourne, but only to make the crowd stay back. Sid said Norton shot Campbell. He claimed Norton was the boss of the gang and backed up Williams's story that Slim had been against the robbery. Williams, said Murrell, was a "weak sister."

Slim Williams was transported from Kingston to London for the trial, which began on October 15. Throughout the proceedings he appeared to be a nervous wreck, while Sid was cool and confident. Their attorney, J.M Donahue, clashed several times with Mr. Justice Wright over statements the defence lawyer had made and the admission of documents from the hearing in Melbourne two years earlier. Donahue still argued that both men couldn't be guilty of the same murder. The judge reminded him that in the eyes of the law when a crime resulted in death all of those who participated in the felony were equally guilty.

The trial was a huge sensation, but the audience in the courtroom was small. Only a select few were admitted, and there were armed guards at every door and window. Outside, thousands of people jammed the streets around the courthouse, eagerly awaiting news of what was happening inside.

On October 18 the jurors retired, and by the next day they couldn't agree on a verdict. The foreman came out and asked Judge Wright if the jurors could submit separate verdicts for the two defendants. Wright said no. The accused were either equally guilty or equally innocent. A day later the foreman announced that the jurors couldn't reach a unanimous decision. They were hung. The judge dismissed them and ordered a new trial for January. It was later revealed that the jurors didn't doubt the prisoners' guilt, but one of them strongly opposed capital punishment and didn't think Slim Williams deserved to hang.

A smiling Sid Murrell told Donahue, "You sure done the trick!" Back in jail Murrell said to Governor Byron Dawson, "My stock's gone up twenty percent. I guess I'll be getting special privileges now after what happened."

The same strict guard was maintained, however. In fact, Sid spent several weeks in the hospital after suffering an attack of appendicitis that almost killed him. The trial date had to be set back until he sufficiently recovered.

This time the two accused were tried separately. Sid went before the court on February 5. The same witnesses who had testified at the first trial that they had seen Sid Murrell shoot Russell Campbell repeated their stories. Sid again claimed Norton had fired the fatal shot. When the Crown prosecutor asked Murrell if the people who had testified against him were perjurers, he responded, "Absolutely degraded perjurers!" It took the jury only thirty-five minutes to find him guilty.

When Sid heard the verdict, his jaws locked on the gum he was chewing and his chest heaved. Then he regained his bravado and blew a kiss to his mother and sisters, who were weeping on their bench. William Murrell was silent but had a white-knuckle grip on the back of the bench in front of him. The old man had already said that if Sid were found guilty he would gladly take his place on the gallows.

The next day it was Slim Williams's turn. Sid Murrell was brought into the courtroom as a witness. He stunned the judge by saying he refused to testify. Sid said that if the court had refused to believe anything he had said the day before it wasn't likely to believe him now. However, he relented and took the stand, stating that Williams didn't have a gun when the gang went into the Melbourne bank and that Norton had threatened to shoot Slim if Slim didn't go along with the robbery. The jury found Williams guilty, with a recommendation for mercy. The judge sentenced both men to be hanged on April 10, the same day another convicted murderer, Clarence Topping, was scheduled to be executed.

Over the weeks leading up to the black day the condemned men didn't sing rowdy songs or stage mock hangings. Now they sang hymns and accepted spiritual counselling. On the morning of

April 9, word came from Ottawa that Williams's sentence had been commuted to life imprisonment. Slim broke down and wept at the news. Murrell, said the newspapers, "smiled grimly." Shortly after 5:00 on the morning of the tenth, Arthur Ellis, Canada's official hangman, entered the cell where the doomed men awaited him. Eleven minutes later Clarence Topping and Sidney Murrell were pronounced dead. Sid's father witnessed the hanging and was one of the men who removed the body from beneath the scaffold. The law still wanted Bill Murrell and Pat Norton.

The trail of the two fugitives remained cold for almost four years. Once during that period London police received a good tip that Bill Murrell was working as a waiter in a hotel in Hudson, New York. The Hudson police were alerted, but when officers arrived at the hotel the mysterious waiter had fled.

London officials said they believed Bill had made at least one secret visit to his family home, but William and Mabel vehemently denied this. The couple insisted they hadn't heard a word from Bill since they had last seen him before the jailbreak. Later events would indicate they were telling the truth.

In January 1928 a man who called himself Cecil Miller was arrested in Los Angeles, California, for car theft. A detective named Samuel Davis decided to run a check on the prisoner's fingerprints. He earned himself a $1,000 reward when he discovered Miller was, in fact, Bill Murrell.

Bill hadn't known about Sid's execution, since Canadian news was rarely reported in the United States. When he was told his brother had been hanged, Bill broke down and wept. "I'm the man you want," he said. "I helped them do it." He made no attempt to fight extradition. "I have to go back sometime, so I might as well have it over with."

Murrell confessed to the bank robbery but insisted he had had nothing to do with Campbell's murder. When a Los Angeles detective pressed him on the matter, Murrell snapped, "Say, lay off me about that! I tell you, I didn't do it. It was my brother's gun. It was his shot that killed him."

While Murrell waited for Canadian officers to take him back to Ontario, he spoke freely with his American jailers. "It's tough about them getting Sidney," he said. "But you know, I'm kind of glad it's all over. It's terrible to be a hunted man. I want to go back to my folks and face what's coming to me."

Bill said that after the jailbreak he and Sid travelled together as far as Emporia, Kansas. There they had a quarrel and split up. He never saw his brother again after that. Murrell told the detectives he had worked for a while on railway construction, but then had gotten into bootlegging at which he had both made and lost a lot of money.

Back in London, reporters asked Mabel Murrell for her thoughts on her son's capture. "When they hanged Sid, I thought the law had had enough," she replied. "But what I think should be done won't be any guide to what will be done."

When Stuart Campbell was asked if he thought Bill Murrell should hang, he simply said, "You know what the law is."

Bill Murrell was brought back to Ontario in early April. To discourage any further attempts at escape while a trial date was arranged, he was lodged in Toronto's fortress-like Don Jail. Referring to the old park on Toronto's lakeshore, Bill told reporters that Sunnyside was the greatest amusement park he had ever seen.

The trial was held on October 15. Slim Williams, now in deteriorating health, was again brought in from Kingston as a witness, and J.M. Donahue was once more the defending attorney. Murrell admitted he and Norton had fired several shots to make would-be captors keep their distance but insisted they hadn't tried to hit anybody. Sidney, he said, had shot Campbell. Banker McCandles identified Bill as one of the robbers who had clubbed him with a gun.

It took the jury more than two hours to reach a verdict of guilty, with a recommendation for mercy. Then Justice Logie sentenced Bill Murrell to be hanged on December 17. Bill turned and smiled at his family. As he was led away, his sisters burst into tears.

Reporters pressed around Bill's parents. "We were Anglicans," Mabel told the *Toronto Daily Star*, "but from what we have gone through, we know there is no God. Sid hanged for a crime he did not commit! Since that, one boy killed by an automobile and another drowned, and now yet another for the hangman!"

"Isn't one life enough to take if they must have it!" the elder William Murrell said angrily. "Is this Christianity? … Call that a trial? It was a parade!" A day later the old man protested that hanging didn't stop bandits. It only made them more desperate, more likely to kill. "It's just the way of an inhuman, bloodthirsty world."

Murrell's mother and father weren't the only people dismayed by the death sentence. Veterans of World War I called for clemency for the man who had been a comrade-in-arms in France. More than 15,000 Londoners signed a petition requesting that the sentence be commuted. Several members of the jury that had convicted Murrell sent shock waves through judicial circles when they stated publicly that they wouldn't have agreed on a guilty verdict had they known the judge would pronounce the death sentence. This admission was unprecedented in Ontario history. Several leading magistrates and lawyers said it was illegal and that it was an "Americanization" of Ontario's justice system. The task of a jury, they said, was to determine guilt or innocence, not influence the sentence. Moreover, jurors weren't supposed to discuss a case among themselves once they agreed on a verdict.

Sheriff D.A. Graham of Middlesex County had worries of his own. The hangman, Arthur Ellis, had an execution to carry out in Vancouver on December 17. If Ellis couldn't be in London on that date, the sheriff would have to hang Murrell, and the thought of that revolted him.

For two months Murrell sweated out what he thought were his last days on earth. As December 17 drew near, he could hear the sounds of workmen in the jail yard building the scaffold on which he was to die. Then, on December 14, Ottawa sent word. Murrell had been granted executive clemency. The death sentence had been commuted to a life term in Kingston Penitentiary. When Murrell was told, he gushed, "It's too good to be true! You aren't fooling me, are you?"

Bill Murrell joined his old pal, Slim Williams, in the penitentiary. The search for Pat Norton continued. On several occasions crooks who were taken into custody were initially thought to be Norton, but their fingerprints identified them as other criminals wanted by Canadian or American police. In October 1930, after a bank holdup in Toronto and a hardware store robbery in Orillia, police officers thought they were closing in on Norton. They even had a photograph of a man they believed to be Norton posing with a young Orillia woman. The man slipped through the police dragnet but soon wound up in an American jail where he was identified as a Detroit gunman named Elmer Giller, who went by such aliases as "Two-Gun Babe" O'Brien and "Honest" John Morten. Canadian police never did apprehend any criminal they could identify as Pat Norton.

Bill Murrell was eventually paroled. He returned to London where he lived quietly. On February 10, 1958, he died of a heart attack while driving home from a grocery store.

17

THE MOREL GANG OF MONTREAL

April Fools

At 2:10 on the afternoon of April 1, 1924, a messenger car for the Banque d'Hochelaga entered a tunnel on Ontario Street East in Montreal. In the car were chauffeur Henri Cleroux and three messengers: Roland Fortier, Maurice Thibodeau, and Lucien Brunet. They had been picking up cash from bank branches throughout the city's east end. In the car were pouches containing almost $250,000 in bills of denominations up to $20.

The chauffeur and the messengers all carried revolvers, but their vehicle wasn't armoured. The bank had ordered a bomb- and bulletproof vehicle, but it wasn't ready yet for service. Bank officials had for some time been anticipating a holdup attempt on one of their cars. Montreal police detectives with their ears to the city's underworld grapevine had heard rumours of such an assault. For several weeks they had kept a number of known criminals under surveillance, and plainclothes policemen in unmarked cars had been following bank messenger cars. Then, two weeks earlier, the suspects had shaken their police tails and gone to ground. Believing their vigilance had nipped the robbery plan in the bud, the police stopped following the bank cars. That would be a costly mistake.

As Cleroux and his colleagues proceeded through the tunnel, they saw two parked cars. The one on the left side of the road facing them was a Hudson touring car. It appeared to have been abandoned. On the right, facing the opposite direction, was a Ford sedan. There was a man beside it who appeared to be changing a tire. The bank messengers had no way of knowing that both cars had been reported stolen.

Cleroux slowed down and swung to the left to pass the Ford. The bank car was approaching the tunnel's exit where the road began to slope up towards street level. Then all hell broke loose!

Without warning the blackness of the tunnel was split by flashes of gunfire. For several terrifying seconds nothing could be heard except the explosion of guns, the crash of shattering glass, and the screech of bullets striking metal. The "thwarted" bandits had taken advantage of the lapse in police security.

A barrage of lead from rifles, pistols, and at least one shotgun tore into the messenger car from both sides and the rear. In addition to the bullets that smashed the windows and burst one tire, another thirty-two slugs pierced the car's body. The bandits obviously had no qualms about killing the occupants.

"It's a holdup!" Cleroux cried. "We're all dead!" He tried to gun the engine. It stalled! The messengers drew their revolvers and fired back at the robbers. (Police later estimated that there were from four to eight gunmen.) Then Cleroux said he was going for help. He swung open the door, jumped out, and ran. The chauffeur fired two or three shots at the bandits before a rifle bullet tore through his neck. Twenty-four-year-old Henri Cleroux hadn't made it ten feet from the car. He staggered a few steps and collapsed.

Roland Fortier later described the gun battle: "Thibodeau, Brunet, and I opened fire on the robbers ... using the dashboard as a kind of shield, I started firing to the left, alternately looking up to get vision and then bending down. We all emptied our guns.... With our guns empty, each of us having fired six shots, the men closed in on us. I felt what I think was the barrel of a revolver just under my right ear, and I was told to throw up my hands.... Thibodeau and Brunet each got a rifle poked in his stomach and each was disarmed and told to throw up his hands. There were four men around the car."

The gunmen were all masked. One of them reached into the car and grabbed the largest money pouch. Cleroux lay bleeding to death just a few feet away.

Suddenly, the bandits were fired on from above. The Ontario

Street tunnel ran under a Canadian Pacific crossover. Railway Detective A. Chaput had been on the bridge when he heard the gunshots. He ran down the tracks, looked over the parapet, and knew at once what was happening. The railway cop opened fire on the hoodlums with his revolver. The bandits fired back at him, but then came under fire from a new quarter.

The sound of shooting had been heard by two or three police officers, one of them motorcycle patrolman Israel Pelletier. When he roared into the tunnel, he saw Cleroux on the ground. Pelletier dropped his motorcycle near the fallen chauffeur and snatched up the wounded man's gun. He emptied the cylinder at the robber gang. One of the thieves had a foot on the running board of the bank car and jerked as a .38 calibre bullet struck him, causing him to fall to the ground.

The tunnel had become too hot for the rest of the gang members. Leaving the remaining money pouches in the bank car, they piled into the stolen Hudson and sped away. The robber Pelletier had shot managed to drag himself into the getaway car.

Pelletier and another constable jumped onto his motorcycle and gave chase. The bandits had prepared for just such an emergency. They had punched holes in the back of the Hudson so that gunmen could fire at pursuers. A volley of bullets disabled Pelletier's motorcycle, though amazingly neither officer was hurt. The policemen fired at the escaping car, but it was soon out of sight.

By now the Ontario Street tunnel was swarming with policemen and curious civilians. The officers found that the bandits had prepared their deadly trap well. The overhead electric streetcar cable had been cut to prevent a tram car from unexpectedly entering the tunnel and interfering with the heist. A pair of chains had been stretched across the tunnel exit to ensure that the bank car couldn't escape.

An ambulance arrived to rush Cleroux to Notre Dame Hospital. He was pronounced dead on arrival. It was a miracle that only the young chauffeur had died in the hail of bullets. Fortier was shot in the hand and would lose a finger. Several bullets had passed through Thibodeau's coat without touching him. Brunet was unscathed.

It didn't take police officers long to home in on the gang responsible for the Hochelaga robbery. Twenty minutes after the holdup they found the Hudson on Everett Street in Montreal's north end. It had crashed into a telephone pole. A witness had seen the occupants drive away in another car that had been parked there. All except one. In the abandoned car, police found guns, boxes of ammunition, and a body sprawled across the back seat.

The dead man with a bullet hole in his chest and a revolver in his pocket was well-known to the authorities. He was a lifelong criminal with many aliases. Montreal police knew him as Harry Stone, but he was eventually identified as Peter Ward. Born in Toronto about 1885, Ward had an international reputation as a bootlegger, smuggler, kidnapper, and narcotics dealer. His rap sheet dated back to 1909. He was wanted by police departments from Vancouver to Atlanta, Georgia. At the time of his death Ward was an escapee from a Georgia prison.

A crumpled piece of paper found in the slain outlaw's pocket led police to a boarding house on Coursol Street in Montreal's west end. In a raid on the property that very night, they nabbed four suspects: Giuseppe "Joe" Serafini; Serafini's wife, Mary; Ciro Niegro; and Niegro's girlfriend, Marie Emma Lebeau. The two couples were counting out $8,000 in holdup loot when the police burst in. Mary Serafini tried to stuff $3,000 into her stockings. Police also found cloth of the same material as the mask that had been around Ward's neck. A later search of the flat revealed a secret cupboard with a stash of $30,000. Raids at other addresses throughout Montreal that night scooped up nine more suspects, including two known hoodlums named Salvatore Arena and Joseph Carrero. Arena and Carrero produced what seemed to be solid alibis and were released.

Joe Serafini, twenty-six, was no stranger to Montreal police. An Italian immigrant who had arrived in Canada in 1907, he had been up on criminal charges twice, one for a robbery at the Lowney Chocolate Company and the other for a payroll heist at the Standard Shirt Company. Both times he had been released due to lack of evidence.

Mary Serafini (née Wright), formerly of Hastings, England, was only nineteen years old, though she told police she was twenty-five. Raised in a devoutly Christian family, she had come to Montreal at the age of fourteen to visit relatives following her father's death in World War I. She liked life in the big city and decided to stay. Then the "Demure English Maiden," as one newspaper reporter called her, fell in with a bad crowd — Serafini and his friends. When an uncle who knew of Serafini's reputation tried to warn Mary away from him, the love-smitten girl had been defiant. "I know he is not any little tin god," she had said, "but I love him and I'm going to stick to him. He'll give up that life for me."

In October 1923, Joe and Mary were married. They spent their honeymoon in England, France, and Italy, allegedly travelling on Joe's cut from the Lowney job. Then, back in Montreal, the rose-coloured glasses were slapped off. Mary discovered that her charming husband was a wife beater. Her aunt tried to persuade her to leave Joe. But Mary wouldn't. "I like a masterful man," she told her aunt.

Ciro Niegro, thirty-five, who sometimes used the name Nierri, was also from Italy, arriving in Canada in 1905. He had seen the insides of jails in Quebec, New York, Pennsylvania, and West Virginia. American authorities had once deported him to Italy, but he had made his way back to Canada. Montreal police suspected him of involvement in several robberies, including the Lowney job and the holdup of a Jewish jewellery store. He admitted he had never done an honest day's work in Canada.

Marie Emma Lebeau had been Niegro's girlfriend for about ten months before the Hochelaga stickup. Apparently, she had worked at least part-time as a prostitute, with Niegro serving as her pimp. She confessed she had sewn the masks the robbers had worn at the robbery but said she hadn't been "absolutely sure" what Niegro's "trade" was. She lost no time in cutting a deal with authorities. In return for the court's protection, she agreed to testify as a Crown witness.

Toronto police told Montreal authorities that two months before the Hochelaga job Joe and Mary Serafini and Ciro Niegro had been arrested in Toronto for illegal possession of firearms. A judge had given them a two-year suspended sentence and had ordered them out of town. Another man arrested with the trio, Sam Behan, was an escaped convict from the United States. He had been shipped back to Sing Sing Prison in New York. There was certainly no indication that Joe Serafini had ever intended to "give up that life" for Mary.

Lebeau added to the Toronto police information. She said the gang had been planning a big robbery in Toronto, but the gun bust and the deportation of Behan had fouled things up. Still, they hadn't given up on Toronto. If the Hochelaga robbery had failed, she said, they intended to go back there and knock off a bank messenger car. The plan was to steal a limousine and load it with bricks to give it extra weight. Then they would use the stolen vehicle to ram a bank car. They expected that the armed messengers would be too badly injured to put up any resistance. Not long after this news became public, Toronto newspapers reported the purchase of an armoured car for the transport of bank money.

At a coroner's inquest held on April 9, Joe and Mary Serafini and Ciro Niegro were held criminally responsible for the deaths of Henri Cleroux and Harry Stone (Ward). While Cleroux was given a hero's funeral attended by thousands, and Ward was laid in an unmarked pauper's grave with a lone Salvation Army captain to say a prayer over him, Ciro Niegro decided to save his own hide. In return for total immunity, he would turn King's evidence and sell out the whole gang.

Niegro gave the police names, dates, and detailed accounts of his own criminal activities as well as those of other Montreal underworld figures. From him police learned that Salvatore Arena and Joseph Carrero, whom they had briefly had in their clutches, had been in on the Hochelaga robbery. Detectives placed suspects under surveillance but didn't want to attempt any arrests until every person named by Niegro could be located. They were afraid that if they moved too soon some of the culprits might be warned and get away.

On April 25, before the Montreal police were ready to spring their trap, the news broke that Adamo Parillo, twenty-eight, one of the Hochelaga suspects, had been arrested in Bridgeport, Connecticut, with a large sum of Canadian money in his possession. Now the police had to move quickly before the alarm could spread. Within forty-eight hours another half-dozen men were behind bars. There would be other arrests before the week was out. Arena and Carrero, however, had vanished. The Quebec government began proceedings to extradite Parillo from the United States.

In all more than twenty people were picked up for questioning, but the investigators' attention was soon focused on five men in addition to Serafini, Parillo, Niegro, and the deceased Ward. Leo Davis, a diminutive young man from Newark, New Jersey, didn't appear to have any serious breaches of the law on his record. He was a small-time punk who was handy at stealing cars and who liked to hang out with hardened criminals. Frank Gambino, thirty-seven, had been in jails in Vancouver, Toronto, and Montreal for petty crimes. In 1917 he had been detained as a suspect in a kidnapping case and then released. In 1920 he had been charged with murder but was acquitted due to lack of evidence. Mike Valentino, thirty-two, had been arrested twice by Montreal police on suspicion of fraud but had been released. He was wanted by police in Detroit on two charges of armed robbery.

Perhaps the biggest catch for the Montreal police was Tony "The King" Frank. Tony Frank, forty-three, had come to Canada from Italy in 1907 and was a big wheel in the Montreal underworld. He had a taste for expensive clothes and diamond rings and was known as a "fixer," a crook with contacts in high places. Tony had been arrested on numerous occasions but had always managed to walk away. All it took was some money and a phone call. He was often seen at the courthouse with a thick wad of bills he pulled out whenever a friend who had run into a little trouble with the law needed cash for bail.

The arrest that was most shocking to Montrealers was that of Louis Morel, forty, the alleged leader of the gang. Morel was a former police detective who had once been secretary of the police amateur athletic organization. As a young man, Morel had been a popular amateur athlete, winning seventy-eight trophies in various sporting competitions. Morel's fall had begun when he was dismissed from the force for attempting to organize a police officers' union in Montreal. Instead of finding some other legitimate means of earning a living and supporting his wife and five children, he had turned to drug-dealing. The once-respected policeman had also taken to gambling and hard drinking. Two years before the Hochelaga robbery, Montreal police had quietly investigated Morel as a suspect in the murder of baseball player Budda Harris, whose body had been found in the river, bound hand and foot. The murder was believed to be drug-related, but Morel's name was dropped from the list of suspects. His share from the Hochelaga job was supposed to be his ticket out of the hell his life had become.

According to the story Niegro told police and then repeated in court during two much publicized trials, it was Morel who first proposed the Hochelaga robbery as one of a series of jobs he had in mind. Using stolen cars, Morel and other gang members had on numerous occasions followed the messenger car as it did the rounds. This enabled them to become familiar with the messengers' routine and to scout the best places for an ambush. Through Tony Frank and his contacts the bandits knew about the police tails on the car. They also knew when the unmarked escort had been discontinued.

There had been two abortive expeditions before the actual robbery. The first time the gang members assembled with the intention of robbing the messenger car they got into an argument over where the assault should take place. Niegro testified, "Some wanted to go by the bank door and shoot everybody." But, Niegro claimed, he, Carrero, and Davis objected to that plan. They preferred an ambush in the tunnel. By the time they had convinced the others, it was too late. The messenger car had already passed that site. On the second occasion the big Hudson touring car had gotten so badly stuck in mud that the gang had to hire a truck to pull it out. It didn't seem to be a good day for a robbery, so the bandits postponed the operation to April 1.

On the day of the robbery, said Niegro, Morel, Serafini, Parillo, and Stone met at the shack Morel had been living in and left for the tunnel in the Hudson. Arena and Carrero, who were apparently a couple of Gambino's thugs, were to meet them there with the Ford. Davis, who had done most of the car-stealing for the gang, was supposed to be the driver, but at the last moment the young American backed out Too many people involved, he said. The bandits were armed with Winchester rifles, revolvers, automatic pistols, and sawed-off shotguns. Some of the weapons had been provided by Gambino.

Niegro's job, he said, was to park an alternative getaway car at the corner of Everett Street and Christopher Columbus Street so the gang could ditch the Hudson. Mary Serafini and Marie Emma Lebeau were to wait at the corner of Belanger and Drolet. After the men switched cars, they would cruise by the corner and pass the money pouches to the women. That way, if stopped by police, the bandits would have no incriminating money in the car.

Besides providing weapons and extra gunmen, Frank, Gambino, and Valentino also promised "protection." Niegro claimed those three, especially Frank, could call on important connections if there were any problems after the robbery. They had a profitable little operation going in which they were paid ten percent of the take from any holdups in exchange for "fixing things" with certain police officials and providing funds for bail and lawyers.

Tony Frank, Niegro said, promised Morel's bunch that if they were arrested he would have them out of jail in no time. He had done it before. The fee to be paid to Frank, Gambino, and Valentino for this protection was $18,000.

To illustrate his point Niegro testified that after he and Serafini were arrested Tony Frank had visited him in jail to assure him he had nothing to worry about. If the case actually went to trial, Tony said, he could pull strings and get an acquittal. Frank, though a known criminal, had used forged papers to get past jail security.

"I don't know any police," Niegro said on the stand. Indicating Frank, Gambino, and Valentino, he said, "But they do."

Niegro also said that Tony Frank had offered his own home as the place where the robbers could meet to divide the money. Frank had said he would hold on to money for any members of the gang who had to lie low for a while. But Louis Morel hadn't liked the idea. He had said they would share out the loot at his place, as originally planned.

After the holdup, when everyone met to divide the spoils, one of the gunmen who had been at the tunnel said that Stone was dead. "What difference does it make?" Gambino had asked. Then they had split up the money, in the words of Crown prosecutor R.L. Calder, "as coldly as a banker counting his cash." Morel, however, had said he would give a full share to the dead bandit's widow.

Niegro claimed all the bandits, including those who weren't at the tunnel, were fully aware of the planned robbery and were conspirators in it from start to finish. That made them all accountable for the subsequent deaths no matter who had done the shooting provided, of course, the jury accepted Niegro's testimony as true.

Although much of what Niegro told the court was corroborated by the testimony of other witnesses, defence counsel Alban Germain said the confessed criminal was lying to save his own skin. The name Niegro, said the attorney, would go into the history books with those of other traitors like Judas and Brutus.

The first trial, which lasted from May 26 to June 7, was that of Joe Serafini alone. It resulted in a hung jury. Six members found him guilty of murder, but the other six would convict only on a charge of manslaughter. The judge discharged them and ordered a new trial.

The second trial saw Serafini, Morel, Davis, Frank, Gambino, and Valentino all in the prisoner's box on a charge of murder. Parillo had been returned to Canada, but his trial was scheduled for a later date. The jury-selection process took two days because defence attorneys objected to so many of the potential jurors. The judge had to send officers out into the streets to haul in men from their workplaces and from city buses before a panel of twelve could be selected.

Security was very tight because court officials and Marie Emma Lebeau had received death threats. Montreal was seething with rumours that mobsters were planning an attack to rescue their colleagues. Constables guarded every entrance, and no one was admitted to the courtroom who didn't have a pass. The trial finally got underway on June 23.

Niegro told his story again and stuck to it through severe cross-examination. This time it took the jury only eleven minutes to reach a guilty verdict. Judge C.A. Wilson asked each of the accused in turn if he had anything to say why sentence shouldn't be passed upon him.

Joe Serafini wept and shook his head.

Frank Gambino said, "All I have to say is that I don't know anything about it."

Mike Valentino smiled, shook his head, and gestured towards his friends as though to say, "They've said it all."

Leo Davis protested his innocence. "There is no justice at all," he said.

Tony Frank begged the court to have pity on him for the sake of his aged parents and his wife and children.

Then it was Louis Morel's turn. The ex-detective spoke in a steady voice. "I plead guilty ... I understand, of course, that under Article 69 of the Code, because I am in on this conspiracy, I am held to be guilty of the murder the same as anyone else, and I am perfectly ready to take my medicine. But I regret to see here, at my side, a man convicted of murder who had nothing whatever to do with it." Morel was talking about Leo Davis. "I think it is an injustice to have brought this youngster here into the case who had no connection with this crime whatever."

When Judge Wilson put on the black cap and sentenced all six to hang, Morel, who still had the muscular physique of an athlete, stuck out his brawny chest. At this show of courage, or bravado, on the part of the gang's leader, the other condemned men somewhat regained their composure. The date for one of the largest mass executions in Canadian history was set for October 24.

The prisoners were lodged in Montreal's grim Bordeaux Jail to await their appointment with the hangman. Joe Serafini and Leo Davis went on a short-lived hunger strike. Tony Frank complained of being ill. Frank Gambino papered the walls of his cell with religious pictures and spent hours on end saying the rosary. Mike Valentino wept day and night and cried out repeatedly that he was innocent. Louis Morel quietly passed the hours exercising.

Throughout that summer of 1924 the approaching Black Friday was a much-debated topic across Canada. Would the federal government commute any of the death sentences, or would all six men swing on October 24? Multiple hangings were rare in Canadian history. During the 1837 Rebellion, there had been a mass hanging of eleven men convicted of treason. In 1881 the notorious McLean brothers, Allan, Charlie, and Archie, and their pal, Alex Hare, had been hanged together in British Columbia for the murder of a constable. But those executions had taken place in rough frontier times. Many Canadians had been highly critical of the parole system for letting "rats" out of prison so they could return to their predatory ways. But in the modern twentieth century it seemed barbaric to many that six men should be executed in a group in a Canadian jail. Young Leo Davis, some argued, was a misguided boy who should be entitled to at least another trial.

Rumours still buzzed through Montreal that hoodlums intended to spring one or more of the doomed men. Security at Bordeaux Jail was beefed up. Even so, on the afternoon of August 25, Joe Serafini made a desperate bid to escape the hangman. It was obvious he had help.

The convicted killer cut through the bars of his third-floor cell with a hacksaw that had somehow been smuggled in to him. He passed through several doors and made it to the outside. Serafini scaled the jail's inner wall and was heading for the outer wall. An inmate looking from a window on the jail's upper floor alerted guards to the presence of a car creeping along the street on the other side of the wall.

The alarm was sounded, and Joe dived under a pile of hay in a pigsty. The mysterious car suddenly sped away. Police later speculated that the men in the car intended to toss a rope over the wall.

For a short time the Bordeaux guards thought Serafini had actually escaped. Then Joe poked his head out of the straw to see if the coast was clear. A guard spotted him and ordered him out at gunpoint. There were no further escaped attempts. Nor did Montreal's hoodlums, many of whom no doubt had been sprung at one time or another by Tony Frank, try in any way to assist the doomed men. They were gallows bait now. If they died, to quote Gambino, "What difference does it make?"

Serafini's near-escape resulted in the firing of two guards and the suspension of several others. Of even greater concern to Montreal officials was Niegro's claim that there were dirty cops on the city's force. As part of an official inquiry, Mr. Justice Coderre went to the Bordeaux Jail to question the men on death row. He didn't get much out of them.

Davis and Valentino denied any knowledge of payoffs to police. Tony Frank would say nothing except "I'm innocent! I'm innocent!"

Gambino asked, "What's in it for me?" When Coderre said he couldn't make any deals, Gambino walked away saying, "Nothing doing!"

Louis Morel, still trying to stand tall in a low place, told Coderre, "I am going to be hanged very soon, and before I am hanged it is not my intention to throw mud at any other family."

Serafini was the most talkative of the six, but his information was vague. "He gave me the names of various persons robbed by him and his friends," Coderre reported. "He claims that an understanding was in force between the thieves, the receivers, and the police, whereby the receivers undertook to take the stolen goods at a certain price, which was to be split between the thieves and the policemen."

Before dawn on the morning of October 24, with Bordeaux locked down like a fortress under siege, Frank Gambino and Louis

Morel were the first to be taken from their cells. The night before, Morel had written two letters. One was a farewell to his children. The other was a prayer imploring the Virgin Mary to forgive Ciro Niegro and protect him from damnation.

Gambino fainted on the scaffold and had to be supported by a priest. Morel, according to a *Montreal Star* reporter who witnessed the hangings, "went to his doom as he went to the tape in many an athletic contest that brought renown to Montreal — head up, chest out, but this time with his lips to the crucifix and the prayer on his tongue: 'Jesus have mercy.'"

The morning sun was still low in the sky when Joe Serafini and Tony Frank took their places on the scaffold and were launched into eternity. Witnesses said they took their punishment "like men." But there would be no more hangings that day. Ottawa commuted the death sentences of Leo Davis and Mike Valentino to life imprisonment. Those two, the government decided, had been pawns in the hands of the other four.

Mary Serafini was acquitted of all charges. She and Marie Emma Lebeau disappeared from the public eye. Ciro Niegro, too, did a vanishing act. Although he had escaped both the gallows and prison, the betrayal of his friends would have made him a marked man in criminal circles. There was a report years later that he had been murdered in Italy.

Police all across North America continued to be on the lookout for Salvatore Arena and Joseph Carrero. In April 1934, San Francisco police arrested a man named Joe Ruggero on a petty swindling charge. His fingerprints identified him as Carrero. After a long extradition fight, he was sent back to Montreal. Following two trials in which juries failed to convict him, he was released in March 1936.

Adamo Parillo was convicted of manslaughter and served twelve years in prison. In December 1936, shortly after he was pardoned, Parillo was gunned down in Saratoga Springs, New York, in what police believed was a gangland slaying. With bullet wounds in his chest and neck, Parillo died on a hospital doorstep, whispering, "Help me!"

Salvatore Arena was never apprehended. Perhaps he lived to enjoy his share of the Hochelaga loot. Or it could be that he shared the fate of Niegro and Parillo and his body was secretly disposed of.

18 LOUIS BEVIS
Shootout in Halifax

*L*ouis Bevis of Halifax, Nova Scotia, said that life never gave him a chance. His father had a criminal record, and in 1913, at the age of fourteen, Louis started down the same path when he was sent to reform school for theft. He escaped a year later, but within a few months he was in jail again. February 1915 saw him sentenced to eighteen months for yet another robbery. In 1916, after narrowly dodging another jail term, Bevis lied about his age and joined the Canadian army. He was sent to France and spent twenty-three months in the mud and blood of the trenches. Lou returned to Canada a decorated soldier.

But Bevis couldn't stay out of trouble. Between December 1920 and March 1922 he was arrested three more times, twice for theft and once for making threats against his mother. In July 1922 he was arrested for burglary in Saint John, New Brunswick, and was questioned in connection with the murder of Frederick Trifts, who was found dead from a fractured skull in his car not 300 yards from the scene of Bevis's crime. The Saint John police were satisfied, however, that the burglar had nothing to do with the murder. A letter written by Bevis three years later would have people wondering if perhaps he did.

Having made himself known to police in Nova Scotia and New Brunswick, Bevis went to the United States, first to Massachusetts where he robbed a family that had befriended him, then to

Caanan, Connecticut, where he got a job in a lime kiln. While he was in Connecticut, Bevis sent a bogus letter to a New York City newspaper in which he claimed to be the sole survivor of a shipwreck. The paper fell for the story and published an article about it. The story came to the attention of Halifax's *Herald*, but the editor of that publication realized it was a hoax and didn't carry it. He concluded that a local boy living "away" was just trying to impress some friends down at the waterfront.

Late in June 1924, Bevis hopped a freight and returned to Halifax. His father had gone to live with him in Connecticut, but the two didn't get along. They had a quarrel, and the younger Bevis stormed out, his father warning him, prophetically as it turned out, that he would get in trouble if he went back to Halifax. It is likely, too, that Bevis knew the police in Caanan wanted to question him about an assault. He had allegedly beaten a man and threatened him with a gun. Bevis later insisted he never assaulted anyone with anything but his fists. Lou Bevis was a small man, barely tipping the scales at 125 pounds, but anyone who had survived almost two years of trench warfare could certainly claim to be tough. Whatever the reason for Bevis's return to Halifax, it was a fateful decision.

Back in his hometown, Bevis hooked up with an old pal, twenty-one-year-old Wilfred Slaughenwhite. The two decided to camp out in the woods near the Northwest Arm on the outskirts of the city and treat Haligonians to a rash of burglaries. With them for this summer adventure were Bevis's fourteen-year-old sister, Muriel, and Slaughenwhite's sixteen-year-old sister, Ethel. Bevis, at age twenty-five, was the undisputed leader of the gang. Just how many break-ins the young thieves accomplished wasn't recorded, but there were enough of them to put the Halifax police on the alert for a criminal gang.

One night, in the second week of July, they entered the house of Captain T.C. Critchley (RCN), formerly the home of Sir Sanford Fleming, the father of Standard Time. Among the articles of loot they carried off were a .45 calibre revolver and a supply of ammunition. The theft of that gun would have deadly consequences for Lou Bevis.

A couple of nights later, on Sunday, July 13, Frank Longard found the foursome on his land near Dingle Road, comfortably settling in with a load of camping equipment stolen from Critchley's house. When Longard ordered them off his property. Bevis stuck the gun in the man's face and said, "Mind your own business." Longard beat a quick retreat and then called the police.

When the Halifax police arrived at the campsite, a gun battle broke out almost immediately, and there would be considerable speculation as to who fired first. Nobody was hit, even though many shots were exchanged, and Bevis and his companions fled into the woods. Police officers recovered the camping equipment and other stolen goods, including some jewellery, and realized they had found the criminals responsible for the burglaries. However, a heavy rainfall prevented them from going into the bush after the suspects.

That night, Bevis said later, was the hardest he had ever spent. He and the two girls became separated from Slaughenwhite. When Bevis thought they had left the police far enough behind, the three sought shelter from the rain under a large tree. The girls lay on the ground to sleep, and Bevis covered them with his coat. Then he went off to get another coat and a hat. Somewhere he found what he needed, then returned to the girls, swimming across Chocolate Lake to avoid running into the police. He dared not sleep, for fear the officers might take him by surprise. Bevis knew the police had identified him, because during the gunfight he had heard a familiar voice, that of Detective James Reyno, say, "It's you, Lou! I knew it was."

Once during that wet, miserable night Bevis saw a bush move near where he and the girls were huddled. He pointed the gun and shouted, "Come out or I'll blow your head off!" The figure that stepped forward with hands raised was Slaughenwhite.

At daybreak the two young men and their kid sisters crept out from under their tree. They were all hungry and wet, and the girls were frightened by the prospect of being arrested. Bevis told them they wouldn't be arrested, because he had a gun. None of the others were armed.

Lou tried to get food at a nearby house, but the woman who answered the door turned him away. At about 9:00 that Monday morning the bandits held up a bakery wagon on Dutch Village Road. Evidently, there was no food on the wagon, so Bevis robbed the driver of $8. He then went to a store at the Arm Bridge and bought some doughnuts and a newspaper. Someone recognized him and said, "That's Lou Bevis. I'll bet he'll be blamed for that trouble last night." The bakery wagon driver, meanwhile, had informed the police of the robbery. The "trouble" of the night before had been a mere skirmish compared to the battle that was about to take place.

Three police officers who had responded to the robbery report spotted the four fugitives, and the gunfight resumed. Again there would be a dispute over who shot first and whether the police even called on the suspects to halt. The officers did admit that their shooting needlessly endangered the two teenage girls.

The group made a dash for the woods across the road from Ashburn golf course, with Bevis bringing up the rear and firing his gun to keep the officers back. One of Bevis's bullets clipped a constable's trousers and skinned his leg. The four made it into the trees as three more policemen, one of them Officer Stephen Kennedy, joined the pursuit.

The Halifax police department at that time didn't provide its officers with firearms. Those who wanted guns had to obtain the weapons themselves. There was no firearms training. Some of the policemen involved in the clash with Bevis that day had only their truncheons. Those with guns had .32 and .38 calibre automatics. No one had a gun as powerful as Bevis's .45 revolver, which meant the outlaw had the advantage in range and sheer stopping power.

The squad of officers spread out and began to move into the clump of trees. Suddenly, there was a roar and someone cried, "My God! I'm shot!" Officer Kennedy staggered a short distance, then dropped to the ground.

Bevis appeared beside the prone officer. He picked up Kennedy's .32 automatic, then ducked back under cover. Later he tossed Kennedy's gun away because it was "too light."

The other policemen rushed to Kennedy's aid. "The dirty coward!" the wounded man groaned. "He got me in the back." Kennedy was rushed to Victoria General Hospital where doctors found that the heavy .45 slug had smashed through a lung. The constable wasn't expected to live.

While the police were occupied with the wounded man, the four fugitives broke out of the trees unseen and crossed the road, heading south. When the officers resumed the search, beating the bushes in an attempt to flush the quarry out, a boy told them he had seen a man crawling along the inside of the stone wall at the edge of the golf course. There they found Slaughenwhite trying to hide under some bushes. He gave up without resistance and didn't lose a moment to tell the police it was his good buddy Bevis who had done all the shooting.

By now every available policeman on the Halifax force had been called in to join the manhunt, including Officer Charles Fulton, who had been enjoying a family picnic on what was supposed to be a day off. Assisting the Halifax police were county constables, railway police, men from the local detachment of the RCMP, firemen, and other civilian volunteers. Even before word got around that Kennedy had been shot, there had been a hue and cry to run a gang of suspected burglars to ground.

The three objects of all this attention were seen near a gravel pit on Long Lake Road. The air was again filled with flying lead. Officer Leo Price had a brush with death when his badge deflected a bullet from Bevis's gun. The slug would otherwise have pierced his heart. Once again Bevis managed to evade capture, but the two girls were caught.

The police officers had been told they were after two men and two women. They were shocked to discover that the "women" were barely more than children, their clothing in tatters and the shoes almost worn off their feet. According to a newspaper report of the time, the girls were taken to the police station with nary a word nor a tear. Ethel Slaughenwhite and her brother, Wilfred, were charged with theft. Muriel Bevis was given over to the custody of juvenile court. Her brother, Louis, was still locked in a duel with the Halifax police.

Throughout the midday hours the police didn't know where Lou Bevis was. Patrols, some of them civilians armed with hunting rifles and shotguns, scoured the roads and back roads outside Halifax. Everyone assumed the desperado would try to put as much distance between himself and the city as he could. Word went around that Chief of Police Palmer had issued a "shoot to kill" order, but the chief later denied he had given such a command. He did give his men the authority to commandeer any car they thought necessary. Dozens of tips that turned out to be false sightings had the police scurrying around on wild-goose chases. Then came word that a postman had seen a man skulking around the grounds of the Robert Simpson factory on Chebucto Road. While the police had been trying to prevent Bevis from slipping out of Halifax, the fugitive had second-guessed them and was heading *into* the city. He had even stopped at the home of an aunt for a hasty glass of milk. Men were quickly dispatched to the waterfront in case Bevis tried to stow away on a ship.

The manhunters began searching along Chebucto Road, always aware that at any moment the gunman could start blasting away from ambush. It didn't help matters that mobs of curious people were out in the streets, watching the real-life drama as though it were some sort of show.

Another tip shifted the hunt over to Quinpool Road, then to Preston Street. Six carloads of policemen, one of them Charles Fulton, roared down Preston Street and screeched to a halt in front of the building where the fugitive had been sighted. Officers jumped off the running boards and piled out of the cars. Bevis appeared from around a corner of the building. He took a couple of shots at the police, then ducked back as they returned fire. His only possible escape route was an alleyway that led to the playground of St. Thomas Aquinas School. Bevis decided to make a run for it, even though he would be in full view of his pursuers. Down the alley he dashed, running in a zigzag. The police let go with volley after volley from their side arms. For the running man it must have been reminiscent of a sprint across no man's land in France except this time the bullets were coming from behind him. By sheer good luck, and perhaps because none of the Halifax police had been trained in the use of handguns, he made it.

The police raced down the alleyway after him, Officer Fulton leading the charge. Bevis reached the playground and kept running. He looked around to see Fulton gaining on him. Bevis stopped, extended his gun hand, and fired. Fulton staggered and fell. Then he got up on one knee and aimed his .32 calibre pistol. Before Fulton could fire, Bevis shot again and put a bullet into the policeman's head.

The twenty-eight-year-old officer was pronounced dead three minutes after his colleagues got him to Victoria General. He left behind a wife and baby. Like Bevis, Fulton had fought in World War I and had been decorated. An editor at the *Herald* remarked on the irony that Fulton should survive the horrors of war only to be shot dead by a countryman. It was initially reported that Bevis's first shot had struck Fulton in the stomach, but doctors discovered only the head wound. Evidently, Fulton fell down because he stumbled on the uneven ground.

Bevis resumed his dash across the playground, heading for Vernon Street. A crowd had gathered there. Someone cried, "Here he comes, boys! Get him!"

"Like hell they'll get me!" Bevis replied, brandishing his gun. "At least not alive!"

No one in the crowd had a gun, and Bevis passed by unchallenged. The pursuers lost sight of him again. Police searched Robie, Carlton, and Summer streets and Jubilee Road but found no trace of the killer.

Then a carpenter who had been repairing a fence in Camp Hill Cemetery told the police he had encountered Bevis in the graveyard. He said the man had come upon him suddenly and he had raised his hammer to strike him. But the man claimed to be one of the posse hunting for Bevis. The carpenter realized that a hammer was no match for a gun, so he didn't try to stop the man.

Officer Charles Fulton is carried away after being mortally wounded by Lou Bevis. (Halifax Police Services)

Police officers and civilian volunteers surrounded the cemetery while other policemen went in to search. At first they couldn't find any sign of the wanted man. Then, late in the afternoon, a resident in an apartment building overlooking the cemetery sent word that he had seen a bush swaying in an unusual manner. A party led by Officer George Fox approached the bush. Fox called out, "Throw up your hands and come out of there, Bevis!"

After a few moments, Bevis emerged from his hiding place, hands above his head, one of them still clutching the .45 revolver. He was limping. A bullet had injured one foot. The wound was painful but not serious. Had it not been for his wounded foot, Bevis said, he would have kept on running. He told Fox, "I could have shot you, Fox. I had another bullet left, but I didn't shoot you because I know you."

In fact, Bevis had three bullets left. He said he had been saving two of them for Detectives Reno and Aitken, whom he accused of harassing him years earlier. The third bullet, he said, was for himself. Once Bevis was disarmed and handcuffed, one of the officers struck him in the face. Fox intervened and would allow no further abuse of the prisoner.

Bevis was taken to the Halifax police station where he signed a full confession. He said he had only meant to wound the officers he had shot to prevent them from catching him. But he repeated his threat against Reyno.

"Yes, by God, if I had seen you I would have shot you," he told the detective to his face. "I am not sorry for what I've done. I'm going to swing for it, anyway, but you are lucky I didn't see you because I was out to get you and I would have dropped you in your tracks. I didn't see you in the woods all day, but I saw the others. Some of them almost walked on me. I am sorry I killed a man who I had nothing against, but what's the use of squealing about it?"

Bevis admitted he alone had done the shooting. After his foot was bandaged, Bevis was taken to the hospital where Officer Kennedy identified the killer as the man who had shot him. The identification was important, because Kennedy was believed to be at death's door. The policeman survived, however, and was a principal witness for the Crown at Bevis's trial.

While Bevis was in jail awaiting trial, he wrote a letter in poorly spelled and awkward English to a Mrs. Mary Golden in Woburn, Massachusetts. Hers was the family Bevis had lived with and then robbed. Now, in a letter dated July 21, 1924, he was asking for forgiveness:

Dear Mrs. Golden:

I am now waiting to die for a double charge of murder. To me come tonight come memorys of the past of things I have done. I want you to know that I am not writing for sympathy or anything like that. But I want you to know I have been a mean devil to you and I am writing to ask if you will forgive me for what I have done against you people — by robbing you of that money and other things which I have stole. I am not able to return anything because I aint got a friend to help me out and no money to return what I have taken but I must say I regret the day I did what I did against you and have never been happy since you were so kind to me and good and I am so sorry that I did it. Please forgive me and say a prayer for I need them. I have been a crook for fifteen years and have always made my money by holding up places of business. I always travelled with a woman, but my sweatheart was in jail and I went to work and was going to reform but she was coming out of jail that Friday and the old game began to come into my mind and I began to think about the girl and what a game little pal she was to me and I had to go back to the old haunts again. I have been a ringleader of a notorious [gang?] ever since I have been able to handle a gun. I have been tried for murder twice before and have won out but I am hard up against it now. I am going to die and my real name is what I want to tell you. It is not Earl Arlington but Louis Marshall Bevis alias Earl Arlington, Louis Butler, Robert Buchanan, Robert Nolan. Those are the names I have went under in different citys. My father was a crook as well he is the man who is responsible for my troubles. If you will answer this letter I shall be very happy. I am sending you

*a piece of paper with the first man I shot and if you wish to
see the rest you can get the Halifax paper in Boston ... so
get those two papers and will see everything and learn who
and what I am but I wish you would write and say you will
forgive and forget what I have done. Please don't say no it
is all I ask and it will be great favor to me.*

Sincere,
Louis Marshall Bevis
Halifax County Jail
Halifax N.S. Canada

Of course, Bevis's jailers read the letter, and the line about
beating other murder raps intrigued them. There was no record
anywhere of Bevis being charged with murder prior to the shootout
in Halifax, so they wondered about the incident in Saint John. It
wasn't possible to connect Bevis officially with the Trifts murder,
and in all likelihood he had nothing to do with it. But a copy of the
letter was read in court and was certainly damaging to Bevis's case.
In response to questions about statements he had made in the letter, Bevis said that fellow prisoners in the jail had suggested as a
joke that he feed Mrs. Golden "a line" and that most of what he
had written was "just bull."

Bevis's trial for murder and attempted murder took place over
four days in October 1924. Mr. Justice Chisholm was on the bench.
Prosecuting for the Crown was Nova Scotia attorney general W.J.
O'Hearn. Bevis was represented by Major J.W. Madden of Sydney,
considered to be one of the best defence lawyers in Nova Scotia.

Madden entered a plea of not guilty and proceeded to rake the
Halifax Police Department over the coals. He acknowledged that
his client had a long record and was "no Sunday school teacher"
but argued that Bevis had fired at the police in self-defence. The
police, said Madden, had "run amuck." The officers had opened
fire on Bevis without identifying themselves and without giving
him a chance to surrender peacefully. They had brought into the
manhunt civilians who constituted a mob. The police had fired "a
ton of lead" at him between Chocolate Lake and Camp Hill, with
little regard for public safety. There had indeed been instances of

police bullets crashing through windows and doors of private residences, though fortunately no innocent bystanders were hurt.

The defence counsellor claimed Bevis had given himself up to Officer Fox because Fox was the first policeman to give him the opportunity. Everyone else, in their zeal to apprehend a gang of burglars, had been going by the rule of shoot first and ask questions later. When Bevis headed *into* the city, rather than away from it, the lawyer explained, he was determined to get to City Hall where he thought it would be safe to surrender to the authorities.

Madden showed the jury the medals Bevis had won in the war. He asked if it was fair for the government to train a man in the use of weapons, send him off to war where his one duty was to kill, and then bring him home and tell him to settle down and "be a good boy, resume the golden rule, and forget all about the nightmare he had lived through."

As for the confession Bevis had signed in the police station, Madden said he had done so under duress. His client was exhausted, hungry, thirsty, in pain, and didn't know what he was signing. Moreover, the police had told him he wouldn't be given anything to eat until he signed the statement.

About the Halifax police station, Bevis himself testified, "I seen a lot of guys get their heads kicked there. I said anything they liked to make them feel good. In a lot of burglaries I served time just because I kept my mouth shut and not because I did them."

Throughout the trial Bevis seemed cool, sometimes even defiant. He had nods and smiles for his mother and old friends among the spectators. When cross-examined by O'Hearn, Bevis was impudent. Questioned about a particular action, he would reply, "What would *you* do?"

Testimony contradicting Madden's arguments came from Wilfred and Ethel Slaughenwhite and even from Muriel Bevis. All three said Lou had been the first to shoot. He had boasted about shooting Kennedy and said he wouldn't hesitate to shoot more cops. Bevis himself said that the police "fired back" in the gun duel, indicating he had fired first. Chief Palmer denied that Bevis had been compelled in any way to sign a statement. He added that after his incarceration Bevis had removed some iron and steel fittings from the door of his cell and had sharpened them. These homemade weapons had been found during a cell search. Bevis explained he had used the sharp instruments to slice bread because he wasn't allowed a knife.

It came down to the matter of the bullet that had killed Fulton. Madden said that a lot of lead had been flying around that day, most of it from police guns. Bevis had a .45. The officers had .32s and .38s. Wasn't it possible that Fulton had been struck by a stray police bullet? Wasn't it even possible that when Officer Fulton stumbled his gun had discharged and he had accidentally shot himself? Where was the bullet that had killed the policeman? The prosecution didn't have it. Dozens of people had seen Bevis shoot Fulton, but now some of them weren't sure what they had seen. A similar situation arose regarding the shooting of Kennedy. The officer had seen Bevis come and pick up his gun, but did he actually *see* Bevis shoot him? Well, no. Therefore wasn't it possible that Kennedy had been hit by a bullet from the gun of one of his fellow officers? Where was the bullet?

The law demanded that a person on trial for his or her life had to be found guilty "beyond all reasonable doubt." Some of the members of the jury felt there was indeed reasonable doubt in this case. They couldn't agree on a verdict. They were dismissed and a new trial was scheduled.

For six days in November a new jury heard the same arguments that had been given in October: that the Halifax police had been overzealous and unprofessional in its desire to catch burglars. Misguided teenage girls had been thoughtlessly placed in mortal danger. Lou Bevis had been running for his life from a mob. He had been seeking the protection of City Hall, understandably terrified to surrender to police officers who were out to kill him.

But this time O'Hearn was better prepared. He had more than enough evidence to show that Bevis had fired first and that the accused had had many opportunities to surrender if he had wanted to. He tore the story about Bevis running to City Hall "for protection" to shreds. Moreover, he had the fragments of the bullet that had been taken from Fulton's head by the doctors at Victoria General and by the undertaker who had prepared the body for burial. They were pieces of a .45 calibre slug, and the only man who had had such a gun on the fatal day was Lou Bevis. The jury returned a verdict of guilty, but with a recommendation for mercy.

The judge presiding at a trial couldn't act on such a recommendation. When a prisoner was found guilty of a capital crime like first-degree murder, the judge was duty bound to pronounce the death sentence. Justice Chisholm, therefore, sentenced Louis Bevis to be hanged on February 11, 1925. The recommendation for mercy was sent to Ottawa for consideration by the federal government, which had the final word in such matters.

Since Confederation more than half of the death sentences pronounced by Canadian judges had been commuted to prison terms, but this time the government wasn't inclined to grant clemency. Nor was it moved by an appeal for a stay of execution sent to Prime Minister Mackenzie King by the Halifax branch of the Great War Veterans Association on February 10. On the morning of February 11, Louis Bevis climbed the steps of the gallows in the yard of the Halifax jail with a cigarette dangling from his lips. He said, "Goodbye, boys," before hangman Arthur Ellis put the hood over his head and the noose around his neck. He never disclosed why he had chosen to shoot it out with the Halifax police over what amounted to petty burglary.

19 ORVAL SHAW
The Mystery Man of Skunk's Misery

*A*s far as being a criminal was concerned, Orval Shaw never rose above the level of small-time thief. Yet, in the late 1920s, this five-foot-five, generally good-natured young man was the object of a manhunt involving hundreds of officers from the Ontario Provincial Police and the police departments of at least ten Southern Ontario municipalities. The incredible chase in which Orval eluded the cops time and time again captured the public imagination. Front-page newspaper articles under banner head-lines chronicled his escapades, and for a while Orval Shaw was an Ontario folk hero. However, though Orval's crimes were, for the most part, petty, his cat-and-mouse game with the police would result in a tragic moment of gunfire and death.

Orval Shaw was born in 1904 in Ridgeway, Ontario, but grew up in the village of Bothwell near Chatham. He was orphaned while still very young and was raised by his poverty-stricken grandmother. Orval liked the outdoors and spent a lot of time prowling around a section of wild country just east of Bothwell. It was called Skunk's Misery. The origin of the name had been lost, but Skunk's Misery was 1,000 acres of bush and swamp with a few convenient dugouts people referred to as caves. Most of the local farmers kept clear of it, but Orval came to know it like the back of his hand. He didn't mind at all sleeping in a cave after a dinner of groundhog meat cooked over a campfire.

One thing Orval wasn't terribly fond of was work. He did occasionally hire out to farmers, and for a time he had a job as a groundskeeper at the Homewood Sanitarium in Guelph, but Orval preferred stealing to meet his daily needs. Shaw would break into homes and shops to pilfer food, clothing, and small items.

Although neighbours found Orval to be a likeable fellow, they couldn't abide the stealing, and in January 1926 he was arrested on two charges of theft. The charges were dropped, but in November of that same year Orval was once again arrested. This time he did six months in the Ontario Provincial Reformatory in Guelph.

Jail didn't cure Orval of his light-fingered ways, and he went right back to stealing. He was arrested again but decided that another stint in the reformatory wasn't for him. On October 27, as he was being escorted to a police car from the jail, he suddenly tore loose from the one officer guarding him and ran down the street while bullets whistled over his head. Orval lost the pursuing officer and fled into the bush. The legend of the Mystery Man of Skunk's Misery was about to begin.

Over the next year the police made searches of the bush but couldn't find Orval Shaw. They discovered caves in which he had slept but couldn't lay hands on the "wild man," as the newspapers were starting to call him. While Orval was on the dodge, his grandmother died. Police watched the funeral, hoping he would make an appearance, but he didn't take the risk.

Orval lived by stealing food, but police were certain he also had friends who were sheltering him. One farmer admitted to the *Toronto Daily Star*: "If he came to my house tonight and wanted a meal, I would give it to him." Despite this display of public sympathy for the fugitive, police became alarmed when a hardware store in Bothwell was broken into and a shotgun and a supply of ammunition were stolen.

Shaw, if it was indeed he who had stolen the gun, had never shown any inclination towards violence and probably needed the gun to kill game. But an armed fugitive was always a concern. People who had made formal complaints against Shaw in the past began locking their doors at night.

Newspapers gave the story a lot of coverage. The combination of the runaround the outlaw was giving the police and the colourful name of his hideout made good copy. Every time there was a bur-glary in Kent County, it was attributed to "the phantom" of Skunk's Misery. The papers even printed a rumour that Orval had joined forces with Pat Norton, a much more dangerous criminal who was wanted for murder. (See chapter 16, "The Murrell Gang: Taught to Kill.") Police officials dismissed this rumour and were annoyed that every time they prepared to send a posse into Skunk's Misery the papers ran a story about it. Orval evidently got word, because when police officers made their search he was gone.

On the night of September 18, 1928, on a back road about three miles from Skunk's Misery, police officers following a tip came close to nabbing the slippery Shaw. As they drove down a concession road, they suddenly found themselves face-to-face with Orval, who was at the wheel of a stolen car. At that moment the police car stalled, but it was blocking the road.

The officers jumped out with guns drawn. Orval cranked the wheel and made a wild U-turn, knocking down 100 feet of fence as he roared away from the cops. The officers opened fire, and nine bullets ripped into the back of Orval's car. One slug grazed the out-law's wrist, causing him to lose control of the vehicle and crash into the ditch. Shaw jumped out and fled into the dark woods.

Bothwell, Ontario, about the time Orval Shaw was the most wanted man in the province. (Marion Matt Historical Collection)

A little more than a month later the police had a lucky break. A Bothwell man reported sighting Shaw at an old deserted house in Skunk's Misery. Bothwell Police Chief Boam and three constables drove out after midnight with the car lights off. They stopped a mile from the house and walked the rest of the way. Three men took up positions around the small frame house to block any attempted escape. When Constable J. Sheff burst through the front door, Orval dashed out the back and found himself covered by the gun of High Constable Alvah Peters.

Orval now faced twenty charges, including one of unlawful escape, and was suspected of the recent armed robbery of a gas station. "I haven't pulled half the stuff you blame on me," Shaw told reporters in the Kent County jail in Chatham. He said that at the time of the local "crime wave," he had been visiting friends in Detroit, St. Catharines, and Guelph. When arrested, Orval had $2.75 in nickels in his pocket.

The authorities made an effort to play down the aspects of romantic adventure that the press had attached to Orval's story. They pointed out that he had been living in a cave "like an animal" and referred to him as a "pest bandit."

At his trial in Chatham in late November, Orval was sentenced to two to four years. The prosecution wanted him sent to the federal penitentiary in Kingston, but Orval's defence counsellor convinced the judge that locking the young man up with hardened criminals would serve no useful purpose. The court decided instead to send him back to the Guelph Reformatory. Orval Shaw had other ideas.

Three days before Christmas 1928, Orval was still in the Kent County jail. He and another inmate, Peter Brennan, were sent down to the boiler room, unescorted, to dispose of some rubbish. There they found a window that wasn't barred. They seized the opportunity and escaped. The chase was on again.

Pete Brennan was a rather pathetic individual. In his mid-twenties, Brennan had immigrated to Canada from England as a boy and had never amounted to anything. His usual routine was to hire out to farmers or work on the lake boats during the warm weather, then get himself arrested for vagrancy before the cold weather set in, so he could spend the winter in jail. Why he broke out with Orval Shaw isn't known, but it would prove to be a fatal decision.

Once again there was a rash of burglaries as Orval and Brennan stole food and clothing. They broke into a store in the little community of Duart and took a shotgun, four revolvers, and some cigars. Police later found the stubs of the stolen cigars in a summer cottage in which the escapees had taken shelter.

While police posses once again swept Skunk's Misery, Orval and Brennan stole a car in the village of Glencoe and headed for Guelph. There was a sudden rise in the reports of burglaries in Guelph and the neighbouring communities of Kitchener, Waterloo, and Elora. Most of the thefts were of food, but an Elora hardware store was missing three shotguns and hundreds of rounds of ammunition.

At three o'clock in the morning, New Year's Day 1929, a constable named Byrne was driving through Aberfoyle in Puslinch Township, south of Guelph. He saw two men standing beside a car at the side of the road. Byrne stopped and asked them if they were having trouble. When they responded rudely, the constable became suspicious and began to question them. One of the men pulled a gun and told Byrne, "Move along or I'll drill you."

Byrne drove to the nearest telephone, and soon the area was swarming with police. In the abandoned stolen car they found many of the items that had been pilfered during break-ins, including a pair of antique pistols. But the fugitives had vanished into the night.

For a month and a half police officers scoured the woods in Puslinch and made return visits to Skunk's Misery. They found no trace of Orval or Brennan. Not until mid-February did they get their next break, one that would lead to tragedy and an angry outcry from the public.

Orval and Brennan had stolen a car in Hespeler and had driven north to the vicinity of Bolsover, east of Lake Simcoe. They broke into a summer cottage and made themselves at home, telling neighbours they were friends of the owner, a Miss East of Toronto. One of the neighbours, however, was suspicious. He wrote to Miss East and sent along the licence number of the strangers' car.

Miss East traced the owner of the car, a doctor in Hespeler, and told him where his automobile was. The doctor passed on the information to police in Hespeler. In the early morning of February 16, Orval and Brennan's holiday was dramatically interrupted.

A party of Ontario Provincial Police officers from Barrie, Collingwood, and Orillia met in Bolsover where the local constable gave them directions to Miss East's cottage. They started down the country road, but when their car became stuck in snow they got out and walked. Before they reached the cottage the officers met two men walking down the road in the predawn darkness. An officer told them to identify themselves, and the pair turned and ran. When they didn't halt on order, the police fired over their heads. The suspects still ran. Then one of the fleeing men allegedly pulled something out of his pocket. Fearing it was a gun, the police fired again. The man staggered and fell with a bullet through his heart. His companion kept running and managed to lose his pursuers in the dark woods. When the officers reached the fallen suspect, they found he had a small billy club in his hand, not a gun. He was otherwise unarmed.

None of the policemen present had ever seen Shaw or Brennan, but word went out to the press that they had killed Orval Shaw. Not until a day or two later when a policeman from Chatham arrived did they learn the dead man was Peter Brennan. Shaw, meanwhile, had made his way to Lindsay where he hopped a freight train and again gave police the slip.

The public was outraged over the shooting of Brennan, who had been considered a harmless vagrant. Newspaper editorials raked the police over the coals for the unjustified use of firearms. The wanted men, they said, were petty thieves, not murderers. Public sympathy for Orval Shaw escalated. He was now seen as a man persecuted by police who had been frustrated in their attempts to catch him.

In their own defence, police spokesmen said they had had every reason to believe the jailbreakers had been armed. Hadn't one of them threatened Constable Byrne with a gun that New Year's morning in Aberfoyle? As for the still uncaptured Shaw, he was, they said, "a baffling combination of criminality, frivolity, and eccentricity." He would rather steal than work and was "a leech on society." Two of the officers involved in the Brennan shooting were tried for manslaughter and were acquitted.

A few days after Brennan's death an open letter to Orval Shaw appeared in Ontario newspapers. It was written by W.H. Golding, the reeve of Bothwell. It read in part: "If you will get in touch with me by mail, telephone Bothwell 521, or in any other way, I will arrange to meet you…. The people of Bothwell know you are not a criminal. We feel that you should not be hunted by armed police…. I want to talk to you, to hear your own story and to help you…. I will not do or say anything to betray you."

Golding's letter drew an angry protest from the police, who reminded reporters that Orval Shaw was a burglar, an automobile thief, and a jailbreaker. Police officials also pointed out that the searches for Shaw had cost the taxpayers a lot of money. But Golding received many letters congratulating him for taking a stand in Shaw's defence, including one from Senator A.C. Hardy of Brockville: "Permit me to congratulate you on your courage in writing an open letter to the man Shaw, now a fugitive from justice."

Orval's case was catching the attention of influential people, but Shaw didn't respond to Reeve Golding's letter. More than a month would pass before the next act in the Orval Shaw drama was played out. When it hit the papers, it was a bomb that enhanced the image of the Skunk's Misery bandit as a folk hero as wily as Robin Hood.

On March 30, 1929, Howard Gumbley, a long-time gardener for Homewood Sanitarium in Guelph, was surprised when his old pal Orval Shaw drove up in a flashy car wearing the uniform of a British army lieutenant. Grumbley walked over to speak to Shaw, who didn't get out of the car. When the gardener asked what he was doing, Orval cheerfully replied, "Oh, I'm just swinging the lead and getting away with it."

Grumbley told Orval that he appeared to be in pretty good health. Smiling like a man who didn't have a worry in the world, Orval replied, "I feel mighty good." Then he drove away. Grumbley went into the hospital and told the chief of staff he had just seen Orval Shaw. Within minutes Guelph police officers were at Homewood questioning Grumbley while others patrolled the streets looking for the car he had described (he hadn't noted the licence number). A roadblock was set up on the highway to Kitchener because Grumbley had said Orval seemed to be heading in that direction.

While police cars were cruising the streets in the vicinity of Homewood, a man believed to be Orval Shaw was in another part of Guelph going door to door on a residential street and posing as a government radio inspector. In those days radio owners had to buy a licence every year to operate radios. Orval was asking people who hadn't renewed their licences to pay him a $2 fee. The scam evidently didn't work, because people knew the government fee was only $1. But the very idea of Orval being so brazen further endeared him to his admiring public.

The following night Guelph police received a report that Shaw was in the village of Eramosa, about four miles northeast of the city. A carload of officers headed out on the Eramosa Road. They hadn't cleared Guelph city limits when Orval's car, travelling in the opposite direction, thundered past them at high speed. The officers tried to give chase, but their car stalled. Orval roared through Guelph, ditched his car on the road to Puslinch, stole another one, and vanished again.

Police soon found the abandoned car. It had been stolen from a Barrie garage that had a supposedly thief-proof lock, and from under the noses of two night watchmen. In the car were two hunting knives and an aviator's helmet.

The police believed that Orval was hiding in the bush in Puslinch Township. They spent a cold, drizzly night tramping through the woods and found nothing. Other officers watched every highway out of Guelph. There was no sign of the phantom.

On April 2, Shaw was seen going into a barn on a farm near Hespeler. When the police arrived, the farmer said he hadn't seen the suspect come out. But when the constables entered the barn, the only evidence they found that Orval had been there was the discarded army jacket. Orval, evidently realizing he had been spotted, had kicked some boards out of the back wall and gotten away.

Constables surrounded the area and beat every bush. They told reporters that a capture was imminent. But once again the will-o'-the-wisp escaped their net. The frustration hardened the resolve of law-enforcement officers to bring the fugitive in. "Orval Shaw and the provincial police are going into a contest with the gloves off," said OPP Deputy Commissioner Alfred Cuddy. "It is now past the joke stage."

The Toronto Police Department sent William Stringer, their top detective, to assist with the manhunt. His instructions were simple: "Get the man!"

By the end of another week, however, the only trace of Orval the officers had found was a tent he had set up in the woods. It was made of rugs and carpets stolen from farmhouses and contained a cot and an oil stove. When police officers tried to question local people, the farmers told them they should give up the search and leave Orval alone. Newspapers derisively called the search through the fields and bush, "The Barnyard Derby."

For weeks police followed up tips on "sightings" of Orval Shaw in Brantford, Chatham, and Guelph. It was one wild-goose chase after another. People joked that the police were "Orval" anxious to catch the fugitive. A dairy company ran a newspaper ad that said Orval Shaw remained at large because he drank its "safe" milk. The public howled with laughter when the press announced that Orval Shaw's signature had been found in the guest book placed in the provincial police commissioner's reception room in Queen's Park in Toronto. The fox had seemingly stood on the threshold of the lion's den!

But while his fans cheered him on, Orval found that life on the run was wearing him down. He decided to contact Reeve Golding. The two men met late in April on a country road bordering Skunk's Misery. Golding told Orval that if he would surrender, Golding and other friends would do everything they possibly could to make things easier for him. The reeve offered to escort Orval personally to a police station to ensure he wouldn't be harmed.

Shaw thought about it, and then to Golding's disappointment he said he couldn't surrender. He was afraid of being given a lengthy prison sentence. Orval said he was going to try to make his way to the United States. The men parted, and true to his word Golding didn't betray the young outlaw.

Instead of going to the United States, Orval remained in the territory he knew, stealing his daily bread. In May he made several raids on stores in the little community of Alviston, north of Bothwell. On the night of Thursday, May 9, he stole a car from an Alviston garage. These thefts would prove to be his undoing.

The Alviston break-ins convinced police that Orval was back in his old haunts in Skunk's Misery. On Saturday, May 11, constables scoured the bush in a fruitless search. Then, hoping Orval wouldn't expect them to return so soon, they tried again on Sunday night.

Two police cars crawled along the narrow lanes that passed for roads in Skunk's Misery. In one was an OPP inspector and three officers. In the other were OPP chauffeur Tom Riding and Alviston constable C.C. Northcott. All of the OPP officers were from the London division.

Shortly after 10:00 p.m., the police spotted a pair of headlights that immediately went out. Riding quickly shut off his own lights and parked his car in a hidden spot. He hoped Shaw didn't realize there were two police cars on the scene. The other police car drove away with its lights still on. As soon as that car was gone, Orval shot past the concealed police car.

Riding burst out of ambush and was right on Orval's tail. Shaw knew how to handle a car, but the police chauffeur was better, and he forced Orval into the ditch. Shaw jumped out and made a run for it, shouting to the police to stay back because he had a gun. Orval was actually unarmed, but so were Northcott and Riding.

Orval fled into the darkness, but Riding picked him up in the beam of a high-powered flashlight and went after him. He tackled the wanted man right by a pile of discarded bricks but found himself momentarily alone with Shaw because he had outdistanced his partner, Northcott. Orval Shaw wasn't going to give up without a fight.

The desperate young man kicked, bit, and scratched. He struck Riding with a brick. When Northcott arrived on the scene, he, too, was struck on the head with a brick Orval hurled at him. Every time the officers tried to handcuff Shaw, he renewed the struggle. The fight ended only after Northcott slugged Orval on the head with his billy club, knocking him almost unconscious. The officers handcuffed the dazed outlaw, got him to his feet, and hauled him back to the lane just as the other police car returned.

The police took Orval to London and eventually sent him to Chatham where he would stand trial. In the meantime the prisoner requested another meeting with Reeve Golding. It was denied. "He had his chance and he didn't take it," Golding stated.

Orval told reporters he hadn't been anywhere near Guelph, Hespeler, or Brantford, but had spent most of his time in Huntsville and along Georgian Bay. He said that after he and Pete Brennan escaped and went north he had made his living as a trapper.

"I was doing fine when the police got after us," Shaw said. "The night that Brennan was shot I had a narrow escape with bullets flying all around me. I was running as hard as I could, but

Brennan wasn't making much good time. Brennan, when he was shot, was running with both hands up."

Orval said he hadn't signed the guest book in the police commissioner's office in Toronto. "I never went near Toronto or the Parliament Buildings. Some funny fellow did that." (He later said an old girlfriend had done it as a joke.)

Shaw now faced thirty charges. However, he was tried on only one count of auto theft, for which he was convicted and sentenced to four years in Kingston Penitentiary. The Crown dropped all the other charges. After serving three years and three months, Orval was paroled on good behaviour. He returned to Bothwell and went to work as a blacksmith and auto mechanic. His notoriety was revived somewhat in 1934 when a Toronto newspaper editor, commenting on the massive manhunt in the United States for bank robber John Dillinger, said it was just like the hunt for Orval Shaw a few years earlier.

Evidently, Orval found old habits hard to break. In August 1934 he was convicted on several counts of burglary and receiving stolen goods. Shaw had been stealing tools and horseshoes from other blacksmiths. A judge sentenced him to another three years in Kingston, and he was again paroled early on good behaviour. After that Orval Shaw faded into obscurity, and Canadians forgot all about the Mystery Man from Skunk's Misery.

20

JOHN DILLINGER
The Canadian Connection

*J*ohn Herbert Dillinger! What Al Capone had been to racketeering in the heady days of the Roaring Twenties, Dillinger was to armed bank robbery in the lean early years of the Dirty Thirties. In less than a year the flamboyant Indiana bandit robbed more banks of more money than Jesse James had done in a decade and a half. And he did it with swashbuckling style, leaping over counters, brandishing a Tommy gun with the ease of a pro, and smilingly telling startled female tellers, "This is a stickup, honey." His carefully planned and efficiently executed robberies showed up Bonnie and Clyde for the rank amateurs they really were. In fact, Dillinger complained that the murderous Texas couple "give bank robbery a bad name."

It was the policy of journalists of the time to "play up" the colourful underworld monikers of notorious desperadoes. Names like "Pretty Boy" Floyd, "Baby Face" Nelson, and "Machine Gun" Kelly made better copy and sold more newspapers than stories about Charlie Floyd, Lester Gillis, and George Kelly. In Dillinger's case the boys in the newsrooms didn't have to use a catchy nickname. "Dillinger" said it all.

In Depression-smothered America, Dillinger was seen as a modern-day Robin Hood, though there is no evidence at all that he ever shared his booty with the poor. Just the fact that he robbed the hated banks was enough to allow a dispossessed and frustrated public to applaud him as an outlaw hero. This was a public that didn't know that all of the money stolen from banks by all of the

Depression-era bandits of the 1930s would represent only a fraction of the many millions of dollars that disappeared in one year through political and corporate corruption. John Dillinger certainly wasn't the biggest crook in the United States, but he was the one grabbing the headlines and the one every cop was after. And as much as he publicly deplored the wanton violence of the likes of Bonnie and Clyde, he himself didn't hesitate to shoot if he felt he was cornered.

All of this made for a thrilling real-life drama that unfolded day by day in the newspapers and the movie-house newsreels. Dillinger was as big a celebrity as James Cagney, Edward G. Robinson, George Raft, and a host of other Hollywood actors who made their names portraying gangsters on film. And not only in the United States! During his brief reign as America's Public Enemy Number One, Dillinger saw his exploits hit Canadian papers, too, especially after he made one of the most spectacular jailbreaks in American history.

Early in 1934, Dillinger was captured in Arizona and sent to Crown Point, Indiana, where he was locked up in an "escape-proof" jail. He soon broke out, using a wooden gun covered with boot polish (not a gun carved from a bar of soap as one story claimed). The outlaw drove away in the sheriff's car and went right back to robbing banks.

Dillinger knew, however, that his career as a freewheeling bandit was almost over. Every cop and government agent in the country was looking for him, and as far as the underworld support system for crooks-on-the-lam was concerned, he was now too hot to handle. There were reports that he had undergone plastic surgery (a painful and expensive procedure in those days), that he had submitted to "burning" to alter his fingerprints, and that he was planning one last big holdup before quitting the United States for good.

The manhunt for Dillinger intensified, largely because FBI Director J. Edgar Hoover was eager to make political mileage out of his capture. On the other side of the oultaw/lawman line, homicidal maniac Baby Face Nelson looked forward to Dillinger's demise so that he himself could have the dubious honour of being Public Enemy Number One. Dillinger and Nelson had worked together but never did like each other. John considered Baby Face to be a trigger-happy punk.

Canadian farmers hated the banks every bit as much as American farmers did, and they, too, thrilled to the exploits of bank robbers like Dillinger. Canada's own "Jesse James," the bank robber Red Ryan, had been in jail for ten years, and neither he nor any Canadians who followed in his errant footsteps would ever fit the Robin Hood image. That was largely because the Canadian media never really tried to buy into that myth. Ryan, after his release from prison, would die ingloriously trying to rob a liquor store.

Dillinger's unprecedented string of robberies and his sensational escape from jail made news well beyond the borders of the United States. British newspapers were asking their American correspondents for all the news they could get on the bandit. The London *Times* ran a headline on its front page: "What Is Happening in America?" Canadian police compared their attempts to track down homegrown criminals to the "Dillinger case." Canadian criminals tried to latch on to the reputation of the legendary American outlaw. A burglar named Leonard Conkwright broke into a Fort Erie, Ontario, house and left his victim a note signed, "One of Dillinger's Canadian henchmen." Conkwright was arrested and sentenced to a couple of years in the Ontario Reformatory.

As Dillinger shot his way out of one police trap after another, Canadian newspapers

Bank robber John Dillinger poses with a Tommy gun and the wooden pistol he used in a sensational jailbreak. The FBI received a tip that Public Enemy Number One was on a Canadian ship bound for the British Isles. (Tony Stewart Collection)

made barbed comments about the fiasco going on in the United States, where one man was making fools out of the police departments of five states, as well as the FBI. A *Toronto Daily Star* political cartoon portrayed Jack Canuck offering Uncle Sam the services of one Mountie to bring Dillinger in. A *Daily Star* editor quipped that every country seemed to be getting a dictator. Germany had Hitler, Italy had Mussolini, and the United States had Dillinger. An editor at Toronto's *Globe* sarcastically reported that American authorities hadn't yet blamed Dillinger for the Great Chicago Fire. Shortly after Dillinger's jailbreak, the *Globe* reported the outlaw had visited his sister in Sault Sainte Marie, Michigan, just across the border from the Canadian Soo. How could so hunted a man be able to drop in on family?

Although the Sault Sainte Marie visit seems to have been authentic, there were, in fact, reports of Dillinger "sightings" coming from all over the continent. The *Chicago Tribune*, expressing a little sarcasm of its own, said that in one day Dillinger was seen buying gloves in Chicago; paying for a car in Springfield, Illinois; buying ties in Omaha, Nebraska; purchasing a bungalow in Mooresville, Indiana; drinking soda in Charleston, South Carolina; strolling down Broadway in New York City; buying a fishing reel in Montreal; and having dinner at a hotel in Mexico's Yucatán.

Then, on May 5, 1934, the *Globe* ran a banner headline: "Dillinger on Canadian Liner?" It wasn't a joke. The story revealed that the U.S. Department of Justice in Washington had received information that John Dillinger had boarded the Canadian Pacific steamship *Duchess of York* at either Saint John, New Brunswick, or Halifax under an assumed name. He was supposedly travelling with a companion, though the report didn't specify if that person was male or female. (Other members of the Dillinger Gang were also on the run, but Dillinger had a reputation as a ladies' man.) The ports of Belfast in Northern Ireland and Glasgow and Greenock in Scotland were notified. Police in those cities were asked not to allow anyone to disembark until the vessel had been searched.

Washington contacted the RCMP in Nova Scotia and New Brunswick. Senior officers in those provinces said it was possible that Dillinger had boarded a ship in a Canadian port, but they didn't think it likely. They admitted, though, that it wasn't their policy to screen passengers leaving the country unless specifically requested to do so, and they had received no reports on John Dillinger being in Canada.

Then Washington asked officials of the Canadian Pacific

Jack Canuck offers a distraught Uncle Sam the services of one Mountie to do what hundreds of American law-enforcement officers had thus far failed to accomplish — catch John Dillinger.

Railway and Steamship Line to wire the *Duchess of York* and inform her skipper, a Captain Stewart. This was done, but no immediate reply came from Stewart.

For twenty-four hours the world waited. Was the captain of the *Duchess of York* silent because he didn't want to arouse the suspicions of his notorious passenger, or was it because he considered the message to be nonsense and not worthy of a response? One Canadian official said that it would be almost impossible for Dillinger to get a British visa. But the bandit had been right at the Canadian border, and forged documents weren't hard for men of his profession to get their hands on. He was already known to have obtained a false birth certificate. It was also stated that for Dillinger to flee to Great Britain was like "running into a cul-de-sac." But Continental Europe was just a train ride and a ferry ride away from Scotland. For a fugitive who had just crossed the Atlantic Ocean, the English Channel would pose no great challenge.

Finally, word came from over the pond. Captain Stewart had ordered his crew to search every cabin on the *Duchess of York*, and every place where a stowaway might hide. John Dillinger, he cabled, wasn't on his ship. When Stewart docked in Greenock, detectives from Scotland Yard were waiting to board the *Duchess* and conduct their own search, but the captain convinced them it wasn't necessary.

American police resumed their hunt for the outlaw, with a specially formed "Dillinger Squad" taking the field. The squad boasted of being armed with guns that could shatter bulletproof glass and kill at three miles. The greatest manhunt to date in American history came to an end on the night of July 22, 1934. Betrayed by a girlfriend, the infamous "Lady in Red," John Dillinger was shot down (some would say "executed") by FBI agents as he emerged from the Biograph movie theatre in Chicago. One month after his thirty-first birthday, America's most notorious twentieth-century bank robber was dead. Or was he?

Some American crime historians have maintained that the FBI bungled the Biograph stakeout, as it had done numerous other assignments, and killed the wrong man. FBI chief J. Edgar Hoover, they say, covered up the fatal mistake to spare his beloved bureau from further embarrassment — and to save his own job. Moreover, Dillinger had been the biggest prize of them all and "bagging" him greatly enhanced Hoover's ruthless quest for power. The arguments by those who support this "conspiracy" theory, while not absolutely conclusive, are nonetheless intriguing. However, Dillinger biographer Tony Stewart (*Dillinger: The Hidden Truth*) dismisses the story as groundless.

In all probability it *was* Dillinger who was gunned down outside that Chicago theatre. But if it *wasn't*, where did the bank robber go? Did the outlaw, as one story claims, assume a new identity and quietly live to a ripe old age in the American West? Or could it be that the most wanted man in America travelled to Saint John or Halifax, boarded a Canadian steamer using false documents, fooled Captain Stewart (or cut a deal with him), disembarked at a Scottish port, and then vanished? It's not impossible, and with desperate men stranger things have happened.

Bibliography

Books

Anderson, Frank W. *The Border Bank Bandits*. Surrey, BC: Hancock House, 2003.

____. "Alberta's First Stagecoach Holdup" (chapter), *Outlaws & Lawmen of Western Canada, Volume 2*. Surrey, BC: Heritage House, 1983.

____. "Saskatchewan's First Stagecoach Holdup" (chapter), *Outlaws & Lawmen of Western Canada, Volume 1*. Surrey, BC: Heritage House, 1983.

Arculus, Paul. *Mayhem to Murder: The History of the Markham Gang*. Port Perry, ON: Observer Publishing, 2003.

Boyer, Robert J. *A Good Town Grew Here*. Bracebridge, ON: Herald Gazette Press, 1975.

Burrows, C. Acton. *The Annals of the Town of Guelph, 1827–1877*. Guelph, ON: Herald Steam Printers, 1877.

Clark, Cecil. *British Columbia Provincial Police Stories, Volume 1*. Surrey, BC: Heritage House, 1993.

Congdon, Don, ed. *The Thirties*. New York: Simon & Schuster, 1962.

Hinton, A. Cherry. *The Yukon*. Toronto: Ryerson Press, 1954.

Johnson, Leo A. *The History of Guelph*. Guelph, ON: Guelph Historical Society, 1977.

Kelly, Nora, and William Kelly. *The Royal Canadian Mounted Police: A Century of History, 1873–1973*. Edmonton: Hurtig Publishers, 1973.

MacLean, Eva. *The Far Land*. Prince George, BC: The Caitlin Press, 1993.

Malcolm, M.J. *Murder in the Yukon: The Case Against George O'Brien*. Saskatoon: Western Producer Prairie Books, 1982.

Miller, Orlo. *Twenty Mortal Murders*. Toronto: Macmillan of Canada, 1978.

Murray, John Wilson. *Further Adventures of the Great Detective*. Toronto: Collins, 1980.

Nash, Jay Robert. *The Dillinger Dossier*. High Park, IL: December Press, 1970.

Nash, Jay Robert, and Ron Offen. *Dillinger, Dead or Alive*. Chicago: Henry Regerny Company, 1970.

Powers, Tom. *Michigan Rogues, Cut-Throats and Desperadoes*. Davison, MI: Friede Publications, 2002.

Rogers, D. Laurence. *Paul Bunyan: How a Terrible Timber Feller Became a Legend*. Bay City, MI: Historical Press, 1993.

Wallace, W. Stewart. *Murders and Mysteries*. Toronto: Macmillan and Company, 1931.

Periodicals

The author found source material in various issues from the archives of the following newspapers: *Bracebridge Gazette, Dillon Tribune, Los Angeles Times, Guelph Advertiser, Guelph Mercury, Herald* (Halifax), *Record* (Kitchener-Waterloo), *Montreal Star, Weekly Herald and Algoma Miner* (Port Arthur, Ontario), *Leader* (Regina), *Globe and Mail* (Toronto), *Toronto Star*, and *Daily Province* (Vancouver).

The author also used, as references, the following articles from historical society publications: the Guelph Historical Society's magazine, vol. XXV, "The Doctor: The Public Career of Dr. William Clarke" by Steve Thorning; the Wellington County Historical Society's magazine, vol. 15, 2002, "Capital Punishment in Wellington County" by Ross W. Irwin; and the Nova Scotia Historical Society's magazine, vol. 44, 1996, "Crime and Society in Halifax, 1918–1935" by Michael Boudreau.